Praise for
The Spirit and Art of Conflict Transformation

We know that conflict has the power to build up or to destroy both people and community. Using the power of conversation, Tom Porter shows a way to build up, a way to turn conflict to purpose, to restore people and relationships, and to build changed community. His book offers both theory and pragmatic ways to do this, all in Christian context. Tom has done both his theological and his professional homework and gives us a way ahead to find JustPeace. It is a gift.

GIL RENDLE
Senior Consultant, The Institute for Clergy and Congregational Excellence

At this stage of human history, with all our societal fissures and deep suspicions of one another, we need to hear yet again that life is interdependent, that we are relational. But we need more; building on that fundamental insight, Tom Porter leads us through an imaginative journey punctuated with probing questions, moving us past rhetoric to the development of more effective practices in the critical work of conflict transformation. This is one of those books that can make a powerful and constructive difference today.

DAVID G. TRICKETT
President, Iliff School of Theology
Henry White Warren Professor of Ethics and Leadership

Drawing on a lifetime of experience encompassing a broad spectrum of work, Tom Porter brings insight and passion to the vision of JustPeace and to transforming conflict and healing broken relationships. He speaks to all who seek to find healing and to flourish in a world where our churches and our culture confront tensions and brokenness far too often.

BISHOP LARRY M. GOODPASTER
Western North Carolina Annual Conference
The United Methodist Church

Good leaders know that conflict is a given in human relationships. The question becomes, how does one best behave in response to this inevitable reality? Without sentimentality or blind optimism, Porter calls us to invite others to a common table and seek ways to restore relationships. Peacebuilding is seen for what it is—careful, prayerful labor that sometimes allows those who are fortunate enough to join the process to see God's activity among us.

PHIL AMERSON
President, Garrett-Evangelical Theological Seminary

Like all meaningful contributions to the field of conflict transformation and faith-based works of the heart, Tom Porter's book is absorbing, revelatory, deeply challenging, and imminently practical. It calls us to our core beliefs as humans and believers and then provides implementing a healing process in the midst of conflict that leads to reconciliation. It is a sensitive and poignant work. I read it in one sitting. This book works equally well in academe as it does as a ministry resource.

W. TIMOTHY POWNALL
Director, The Pacis Project in Faith Based Diplomacy
Pepperdine University School of Law
Senior Fellow, The International Center for Religion and Diplomacy

Tom Porter is a spiritual guide for all who long to think, live, and lead as peacemakers. This book is full of wisdom, resources, images, and processes for conflict transformation. It will equip you to live through conflict with gentleness and courage and hope.

BISHOP HOPE MORGAN WARD
Mississippi Annual Conference, The United Methodist Church

This book is a very important contribution to the literature on conflict transformation and circle process because it combines a practical analysis of conflict and conflict resolution process with a discussion of spiritual grounding in a Christian framework. I love the circle process, and it is engaging for me to look at circles through the lens of Christian teachings. The discussion of covenants and appreciative inquiry will be useful to circle practice.

KAY PRANIS
Circle Trainer and Practitioner

Tom Porter's book provides a comprehensive examination of conflict transformation. Theory and practical guidelines are interspersed with stories from Tom's wealth of experience and research. Laity and clergy, experienced conflict transformation practitioners as well as novices will find this book informative and inviting.

BISHOP SUSAN W. HASSINGER
Bishop-in-Residence, Boston University School of Theology

As the tensions in our world mount and the civility of society is tested, Tom Porter's guidance in *The Spirit and Art of Conflict Transformation* offers theological grounding and practical steps toward living in right relationship. There is no magic formula for transforming conflict, but there are actions we can take. Tom's work challenges us and guides us into a better future.

BISHOP HEE-SOO JUNG
Chicago Episcopal Area, The United Methodist Church

Tom Porter has been an important teacher to all of us in the conflict transformation field. Working from a deep grounding in his Christian faith, he has introduced a lot of us to the promising legal horizon of restorative justice. He has built his practice of peacebuilding on radical respect for the other person. With his superb emphasis on bringing the conflict to the sacramental table, his book will be of great value to anyone striving, in faith, for justice and peace.

RAYMOND G. HELMICK, SJ
Instructor in Conflict Resolution
Department of Theology, Boston College

The Spirit and Art of Conflict Transformation

Creating a Culture of *JustPeace*

Thomas Porter

UPPER
ROOM BOOKS®
NASHVILLE

LIBRARY OF CONGRESS CATALOGING-IN-PUBLICATION DATA

Porter, Thomas W.
  The spirit and art of conflict transformation : creating a culture of JustPeace / Thomas Porter.
    p. cm.
  Includes bibliographical references (p.   ).
  ISBN 978-0-8358-1026-5
  1. Conflict management—Religious aspects—Christianity. 2. Peace—Religious aspects—Christianity. I. Title.
  BV4597.53.C58P68 2010
  261.8'73—dc22

                                                                2010010829

To my wife, Zozie,
who taught me how to
live well and joyfully together in peace.

CONTENTS

PROLOGUE

The Great Adventure

Exploring the frontiers of relational life is the great challenge and adventure of our time. How shall we live together? How can we break the cycles of injury, retribution, and violence? How might we flourish together? How do we create a culture of *justpeace* in our relational life?[1] In the midst of this deeply conflicted relational world, we are called to be reconcilers, to be a mediating presence, to be co-creators of a culture of shalom, a culture of *justpeace*. This call is, indeed, a challenge and a great adventure.

The Stakes

The stakes have never been higher. We just completed the most violent century in history. Our present century was birthed in violence. The stakes are high for the church as well as the world. A recent study reports that the greatest predictor of church decline is destructive conflict.[2] We are witnessing on the front pages of our papers how religion can be a source of conflict. In the story of Cain and Abel, we are told the first recorded act of worship led to the first murder (Gen. 4:3-8). At the very beginning of the biblical story, we see that religion can be a source of conflict.

What we believe about God and how we practice our religions is more important than ever to the peace of the world, to God's shalom. As religious people, in an age of weapons of mass destruction, we cannot allow our religions to be sources of conflict. For the sake of the world, for heaven's sake, we need to discover the resources of peace in our religions and make them our practice. We need to move the good news of reconciliation and the call to be reconcilers to the center of our self-understanding as people of faith. We also need to train our members in the practical skills and disciplines that would enable them to be reconcilers. Imagine with me the difference we might make in this world if every church became a neighborhood reconciliation center.

The Journey

I have participated in this adventure and journey as a trial lawyer, as a minister, and as a mediator. While working as a trial lawyer, I became aware of the problems caused by our adversarial retributive system, in which we see ourselves as opponents fighting for our version of the truth, with the goal to punish the loser in this battle. I also served for twenty-three years as a lawyer for the United Methodist Church. During that time, I participated in several church trials, which utilize a system similar to that of the secular courts. As a minister, I have experienced the adversarial retributive model in conflicts within the church, including the way we deal with our theological differences. I began to see the adversarial retributive system of our courtrooms as the model for most of our dealings with differences, conflict, and harm. In my experience, this system does not restore relationships, develop community, or encourage the telling of the truth, especially the truth that heals. In fact, I have seen how destructive this system can be.

I sought a better way—a more constructive way, a more biblical way, a more authentic way of living out our calling to be ministers of reconciliation (2 Cor. 5:17-19). This journey led me from the courtroom to tables of conversation, dialogue, and mediation. As a mediator, I learned to engage conflict and address harm by working toward restructuring relationships and empowering participants to solve their own problems and transform their conflicts. I will never forget the feeling after I facilitated my first mediation. It was truly a spiritual experience. I felt that I had found my authentic self, free to be empathetic and compassionate to both parties. I marveled at the parties' ability to resolve their own conflicts and to come to a better place in their relationship.

A significant part of my journey took place in South Africa, where I studied the Truth and Reconciliation Commission. In South Africa, I felt as if I had "come home." Here an understanding of the relational nature of life came alive through the African concept of *ubuntu*: we are who we are because of our relationships. When I dehumanize you, I dehumanize myself. We are interconnected and interdependent with one another and with the whole web of life. It is all about relationships! I saw the power in telling and hearing each other's stories. I witnessed the essential practice of forgiveness. I also discovered a new understanding of justice, restorative justice, which moves us from a narrow focus on punishing offenders to "a process to involve, to the extent possible, those who have a stake in a specific offense and to collectively identify and address harms, needs, and obligations, in order to heal and put things as right as possible."[3]

More recently I have worked with the JustPeace Center for Mediation and Conflict Transformation of the United Methodist Church and with Boston University School of Theology, helping to develop, or, more accurately, discover the theology, theory, and practice of effective faith-based conflict transformation. Among the lessons from working with the church has been the power of the circle process (explored in Part II), which incorporates these elements:

- the recognition of sacred space through ritual,
- a relational covenant to guide how we treat one another,
- a talking piece to give everyone voice and promote good speaking and good listening, and
- a circle of collective wisdom where everyone is equally responsible for the outcome.

This book reports on my journey and is an invitation to conversation and to sharing what we all have learned, because we all are experienced in dealing with conflict. We have all known destructive conflict and have the wounds to prove it. I write out of gratitude for what I have learned on the way from others, out of humility for what I am still learning, and out of wonder and awe at the power of human beings to come together to talk about difficult issues, find healing and even reconciliation.

Much of what I have learned is summed up in the potential of conversations—simple, honest conversations about things that matter.

Meg Wheatley, who consults on how to create organizations where people are valued, says such conversations can transform the world.[4] Jonathan Sacks, the Chief Rabbi of the United Hebrew Congregations of the [British] Commonwealth, says, "The greatest single antidote to violence is conversation, speaking our fears, listening to the fears of others, and in that sharing of vulnerabilities discovering a genesis of hope."[5] In part, this book is a call to revive the dying art of conversation in our homes, in our churches, in the arena of politics. Without such conversation, we have no chance of conflict transformation or of peace.

I should note that I write from the perspective of one who is trying to follow the way of Jesus and who has grown up in the United Methodist Church. I find the books of my Jewish and Muslim friends are most helpful to me when they speak deeply from their own traditions. I have followed this practice.

Cultures have different ways of peacebuilding. I am sensitive to this reality and recognize that this book and my journey have come out of my experiences as a white male living in the United States. I ask you to make the translations into your own cultural context and ways of bringing peace to a conflict.

The Metaphor of the Well

The metaphor of the well serves to both illustrate and deepen understanding of conflict transformation and the spiritual resources on which we can draw. A well is not a well without the gift of water, but it is also not a well without human construction. The metaphor of the well flows through the chapters.

I invite you to discover and create a well in your life and in your community, to allow your well to fill with life-giving waters, to be well prepared, so you can be well and be a well for others.

The whole book is about how we can all be well together, experiencing healing in our relationships, reconciliation and "holy communion" through the process of creating a common well together, experiencing the well as sacred relational space, appreciating the abundant life-giving waters, going beneath the surface to the deep waters, and drinking deeply the healing waters. My hope is that we can find personal and communal wellness.

Overview of the Book

The Spirit and Art of Conflict Transformation is an overview of the theology, theory, and practice of conflict transformation. When I speak of "conflict transformation," I am talking about something more than conflict management or conflict resolution. The goal of conflict transformation, as Ron Kraybill explains, "is not only to end or prevent something bad but also to *begin* something new and good. Transformation asserts the belief that conflict can be a catalyst for deep-rooted, enduring, positive change in individuals, relationships, and the structures of the human community."[6]

For me, the work of conflict transformation is not the work of putting Band-Aids on the wounds of conflict, or responding to conflict like a fire fighter. This work is about a way of life and the transformation of our culture to a culture of *justpeace*. The book is divided into two parts: the first about preparing ourselves, and the second about how we engage others in conflict transformation.

Part I. How can we, as Gandhi stated, be the change we want to see in this world? We need to begin with the one person over whom we have some control so we can be a peaceful presence in the room. We also need to coach others on how to prepare themselves so they can resolve their own conflicts.

Chapter 1. The starting point is our attitude toward conflict. Instead of viewing all conflict as negative or destructive, we can see conflict as a natural part of God's creation, necessary for constructive change, growth, and revelation. This conversion ultimately is an act of faith.

Chapter 2. In dynamic relation with the change in our attitude is our theology, which is the critical foundation and empowerment for all our work. Our theology matters! Through biblical and theological reflection, we will study the relational nature of creation; a God who loves difference, and who creates and enables relationship and the unity of all creation; a God who forgives and reconciles and calls us to be reconcilers; and practical guidance for the work of reconciliation as described by Jesus in Matthew 18.

Chapter 3. We need more than a positive attitude and a theology of peace. We also need skills. Foremost among the relational skills are listening for understanding, speaking the truth in love, using our imagination, and offering forgiveness. We will engage these skills as essential life skills, as well as spiritual practices.

Chapter 4. Part I concludes with an exploration of the character and values of peacebuilders as well as the role we can and should play. A peacebuilder is not a fixer but a mediating presence, a person with the courage to bring people with differences together, creating a space that encourages openness to the Spirit and to one another's stories, so they can solve their own problems and find healing together.

Part II. The primary purpose of preparing ourselves is for engaging others.

Chapter 5. The heart and soul of good process is enabling, in the midst of conflict, honest conversation about things that matter, moving away from adversarial to collaborative processes. This chapter examines the theory of conflict transformation, focusing on an in-depth study of one such process, the circle process.

Chapter 6. Ritual recognizes the space of conflict transformation as sacred space, creating "order, community, and transformation" and helping us deal with our "liminality" in conflict, feeling betwixt and between, as we journey into the unknown to create a new relationship. A relational covenant defines how we are to treat each other in any engagement and draws on the understanding of "covenant" in the Bible. Both are important to peacebuilding in general and are basic to the circle process.

Chapters 7–9. These three chapters reflect the three most important movements in peacebuilding and in the conversation of the circle: appreciative inquiry, interest-based mediation, and restorative justice. The first movement, in most situations, is to share and build on the positive and best in all the parties—peak experiences, grace-filled movements, and dreams of a preferred future. This movement is informed by the field of appreciative inquiry, a methodology of searching for the positive core in the actual experiences of individuals and groups. A focus here is on the role of questions, inspired by Jesus (the one "who knows how to ask questions"), and the Quaker clearness committee. The second movement is informed by interest-based mediation, moving from positions to interests and needs, generating and evaluating options to meet those needs, and coming to consensus in an agreement that is wise. The third movement recognizes that in every conflict there is harm that needs to be addressed. We will study the way restorative justice deals with harm, accountability, and healing.

Chapter 10. All our work in conflict transformation is to be well together. This process is more than just addressing a single conflict. It is about a way of life, creating a culture of *justpeace*, which for me is most fully expressed and experienced at the Table of Holy Communion.

The Work: Improvisational, Challenging, and Deeply Spiritual

The work of conflict transformation is best described as the art of improvisation. Human interaction cannot be programmed, and there is no script for this journey. We need to be fully present and attentive to the moment, being agile, creative, and spontaneous, willing to take risks. Improvisation, however, is built on structure, skill, and discipline. In this book, we are discussing the processes, the skills, the disciplines that will free us to improvise, as we find our own authentic style of doing this work.

We also need to recognize from the beginning that relationships are not easy. Life in community is challenging and we will not achieve reconciliation in every broken relationship. I was profoundly relieved by a sermon on Jacob and Laban (Gen. 29–31). Jacob had reasons to be angry with his father-in-law, Laban. He worked seven years for the opportunity to marry his beloved, only to have his father-in-law present him with her sister under the cover of darkness. He then had to work for another seven years to win the woman he loved. To say there was conflict between Jacob and Laban is an understatement. Finally, Jacob felt he should flee. Laban's armies pursued him. It appeared violence was imminent. However, Laban and Jacob worked out an understanding. They built two monuments to each of their gods and guaranteed each other safety throughout the cosmos, with these two monuments as the epicenter. There was no kissing or hugging or reconciliation. What they achieved, however, was significant. This story has been important to me, as I have not been able to achieve full reconciliation in some of my own relationships.

Jacob then went on to meet Esau. He had every reason to believe that violence would ensue. However, Esau saw his brother, embraced him, and they wept together. There is nothing more sacred and powerful than such an experience. We hope and work for reconciliation, but we need to appreciate and affirm each step on the way to reconciliation. As my professor Daniel Day Williams said, "Love does not resolve every conflict. It accepts conflict as the arena in which the work of Love is to be done."[7] This is deeply spiritual work! Welcome to the adventure and to the journey.

This book is the collected wisdom I have received from many companions on this journey—too many to name. I do need to acknowledge my fellow staffers at JustPeace:[8] Stephanie Hixon, Mark Mancao, and Adam Bray; the JustPeace board and network of practitioners; my fellow teachers in the Religion and Conflict Transformation Program at Boston University School of Theology:[9] Rodney Petersen, Father Ray Helmick, Dean Mary Elizabeth Moore, Shelly Rambo, Liz Parsons, and Bishop Susan Hassinger; our teaching assistants: Nicole Johnson, Shandi Mawokomatanda, Vincent Machozi, and Tasi Perkins; and my students who have critiqued and improved this book.

PART I

Preparing Ourselves for Conflict Transformation

ONE

Changing Our Attitude toward Conflict

Create a well, not a wall.

∽◎◟

*Create in yourself an openness to conflict as a natural
and necessary part of God's creation, an opportunity
for growth and revelation.*

Our transformation begins with our attitude toward conflict, the way we look at conflict and respond to conflict. Our attitude frames our response to conflict and determines whether it becomes destructive or constructive.

My wife and I were playing tennis against my wife's sister and her husband. My sister-in-law called one of my wife's shots out, and my wife thought the shot was in. My sister-in-law turned to me and asked me what I thought, at which point my wife said, "Don't ask Tom. He doesn't like to deal with conflict." Though I have spent my whole professional life dealing with conflict as a minister, trial lawyer, and mediator, I have learned, thanks to my wife, that I still have work to do to create a healthier attitude toward conflict. My wife was reminding me that it is easier to deal with another's conflicts than with your own.

Adopting a constructive attitude involves understanding conflict as natural and necessary within God's creation. More importantly, it involves dealing with our own emotional response, which requires a radical faith. Conflict is where the rubber of faith meets the road of life. Do we believe in our bones the Word of God, "Be strong and courageous; do not be frightened or dismayed, for the LORD your God is with you wherever you go" (Josh. 1:9)?

Our Attitude toward Conflict

Take a few minutes and write down all the words that pop into your mind when you think of conflict. When you look at your list, are most of the words negative? This exercise always generates words such as: Fear, Anxiety, Anger, Harm, Pain, Wounds, Violence, War. Our typical attitude toward conflict is a negative one—conflict is bad, wrong, or inevitably destructive. A negative attitude appears to be our default position in response to conflict.

Let's be realistic. The truth is, conflict can be negative. Conflict can be destructive and involve all of these negative experiences and emotions on our list. We all have the wounds to prove it. Destructive conflict is very costly—to relationships, to financial and human resources, to missed opportunities, to truth and justice, and to physical and mental health. The question we face is whether we can see conflict as potentially positive. I believe such an attitude will lead to less destructive and more constructive outcomes.

The Response of a Negative Attitude

Before turning from our default position, think about how we typically respond to conflict. Where would you place yourself on a spectrum where one end of the spectrum is *flight or avoidance* and the other end is *fight*? How do you normally respond to conflict?

AVOIDANCE ———————————————— FIGHT

Then think about why you find yourself on this particular point of the spectrum. What experiences have generated this response?

Now place your faith community on the spectrum. How does your congregation deal with conflict? Do you find the community's general response to be avoidance?

Experience teaches that a negative attitude leads to negative responses: defensiveness, anxiety, and fear, and to the fight-or-flight response to the perceived threat. Anxiety can lead to fear, and fear to anger, and anger to violence. Reinhold Niebuhr observed that "anxiety is the internal precondition of sin."[1]

In the world of communal anxiety, as Walter Wink has demonstrated, the most enduring idol is the myth of redemptive violence, the belief that violence or force will save us.[2] As Wink points out, we see this in cartoons, in video games, in our defense expenditures and use of retribution and retaliation as our primary response. Jesus, on the other hand, took the way of the Cross, where violence was exposed and defeated.

The invitation of this first chapter is to *create a well, not a wall*. We often create walls we then fight to maintain or walls we hide behind. We do not have to go any further than the news headlines for examples. The world celebrated when the Berlin wall came down. Now we are in the wall-building business, for example, in Israel and on the southern border of the United States. As Robert Frost says, "Something there is that doesn't love a wall."[3] We know God does not like walls. Jesus died to break down the dividing walls of hostility (Eph. 2:14). Walls are a physical confession of sin. Walls do not make good neighbors. We need to ask ourselves what we are walling in and walling out. We also need to remember the most powerful walls are invisible, in our minds. What might it mean to create a *well* in the midst of conflict, not a *wall*?

Conflict as Natural and Necessary

Let us begin with a working definition of conflict: *Conflict is the result of differences that produce tension.* We live in a world of differences: different people, different cultures, different religions, and different opinions, for example. Difference is a part of life, part of the created order. We also know viscerally what is meant by tension. A sense of alertness and challenge are present. Something demands our attention. Tension in one's muscles is essential to any movement. The ultimate state of lack of tension is death. Tension is not by definition negative or positive. It is both natural and necessary.

Is conflict natural? God created this world with no two snowflakes alike and no two human beings alike. Everyone is unique. God adds to this incredible world of difference the freedom to make choices. Then God put us all into relationship with one another. We are all interconnected, interdependent. What arises naturally from this reality? Yes, conflict! It is part of the created order, which God declares "very good" (Gen. 1:31).

Is conflict necessary? All is not well with our world. We find injustice, oppression, and evil, which we need to oppose, and, in fact, are called to oppose. Has there ever been any injustice, for example, that has been addressed without conflict? Conflict is necessary to engage injustice, oppression, and evil and is a source of energy to do so. When we see conflict, one of our first responses can be, "Congratulations! You are alive and dealing with an important issue." In conflict, we find the energy to change patterns, structures, and people and to improve all three. To transform conflict is to work for right relations, shalom, or *justpeace*.

Often a constructive response will first heighten conflict before dialogue and mediation can begin. The following chart by Adam Curle, a Quaker peacemaker, offers a visualization:[4]

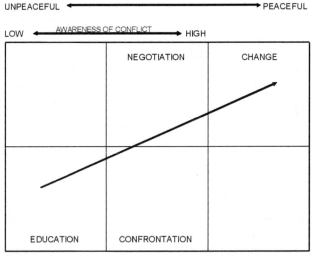

--from *Making Peace* by Adam Curle

When awareness of conflict is low and/or a power imbalance exists, education or consciousness raising is necessary. We saw this reality during the civil rights movement in the United States. Consciousness raising leads to confrontation, increasing the awareness of the conflict, especially among the more powerful. The confrontation, which is envisioned as nonviolent, also creates a new sense of power among those who felt powerless, which moves the conflict toward a more balanced sense of power. Once awareness of the conflict increases and power becomes more balanced, the parties to the conflict can come to the table to negotiate or mediate a sustainable peace.

A Constructive Response to Conflict

We know that many of us find ourselves on the avoidance end of the spectrum. Others find, for a variety of reasons, that their primary response is to fight. We need to be aware of our default positions. But regardless of our default positions, we all need to learn how to engage conflict in a constructive way.

Like most individuals, faith communities usually adopt the default position of avoidance.[5] Often faith communities assume their community should not have any conflict. This assumption leads to hiding conflicts, covering them up or stifling them. What is unnamed and unengaged lies just beneath the surface. The conflict gets worse until it explodes in very destructive ways. We must name and engage conflict to heal and transform our communities and ourselves. Some minor situations can be overlooked, but any significant conflict needs to be engaged, so that it does not become destructive.

How can we be constructive? Think of the times you have engaged a conflict and been successful in doing something constructive. What did you learn?

We can learn from the example of Jesus. As Jesus approached Jerusalem for Passover, he knew he was going to face religious and political leaders who wanted to kill him. He did not head for the hills to avoid the conflict. Nor did he join up with the Zealots to fight. Instead, he mounted a donkey and rode into the eye of the storm. Out of Jesus' and the disciples' experience of the events between the entry into Jerusalem and the empty tomb came the greatest revelations of our faith (Mark 11–16).

We can learn from the early church. In Acts 6:1, "the Hellenists complained against the Hebrews because their widows were being neglected in the daily distribution of food." The members of the community did not avoid the problem, but came together and addressed the issue to the satisfaction of all. In Acts 15 we learn how members of the early church, in the midst of significant theological and scriptural conflict, had the courage to come together, name the conflict, open themselves to hear each other, discern the will of God, come to consensus, and enlarge the covenant to include uncircumcised Gentiles.

We can choose to be constructive. It is our choice. We can choose to create a well, not build a wall.

A Call to Conversion, Trust, and Faithfulness

Our attitude toward conflict is a matter of faith. Do we believe God is present with us in our conflicts? Do we believe that where two or three are gathered to transform conflict Jesus is present? Do we believe God was on the cross, the ultimate image of conflict and of love and solidarity in the midst of conflict? Do we believe in the resurrection, that God is victorious over the powers of violence and death?

In Matthew 18:20, we read, "For where two or three are gathered in my name, I am there among them." Chapter 2 addresses this seminal chapter in Matthew on conflict transformation, a chapter that begins with a conflict over power and ends with a conflict over money. The whole chapter frames how we are to deal with conflict and the consequences of not following a restoring or reconciling path. This scripture is not about a gathering for a potluck, but about the presence of God in the midst of conflict. We are not alone when dealing with conflict. God is present with us. Since God is present with us, we are told we need not fear.

Neuroscientists report that the brain's fear circuitry is more powerful than the brain's reasoning faculties. The amygdala, the most primitive part of the brain, evolved to warn us of life-endangering situations. It is the hardwiring for the "flight or fight" response. Parker Palmer, the Quaker sociologist and teacher, comments:

> When the primitive brain dominates, Christianity goes over to the dark side. Churches self-destruct over doctrinal differences, forgetting that their first calling is to love one another. Parishioners flock to preachers who see the anti-Christ in people who do not believe as they do. Christian voters support politicians who use God's name to justify ignoble and often violent agendas. When the primitive brain is in charge, humility, compassion, forgiveness, and the vision of a beloved community do not stand a chance. . . . Learning how to hold life's tensions in the responsive heart instead of the reactive

primitive brain is key to personal, social, and cultural creativity: rightly held, those tensions can open us to new thoughts, relationships, and possibilities that disappear when we try to flee from or destroy their source.[6]

Conflict can drive us to fear and to acting as if God does not exist, but conflict can also drive us to our knees, to faith. In my experience, conflict can help me understand, like nothing else, my dependence on something beyond myself, and my interdependence with others—in short, my need for assistance from God and neighbor. In conflict, I learn to depend on the resources and power of the Spirit in new ways. Conflict opens me up to know God in fresh and powerful ways. The more I work with conflict the more I am aware that this is where God is most fully present. We will spend the next chapter on the experience of God and what God teaches us and empowers us to do.

The Way to God Is through the Enemy

The "enemy" is the ultimate challenge to a constructive attitude toward conflict. What if we believed that the "enemy" was an opportunity to see ourselves, our world, and even our God in new ways? This belief would significantly change the way we approach conflict. Jesus says:

> You have heard that it was said, "You shall love your neighbor and hate your enemy." But I say to you, Love your enemies and pray for those who persecute you, so that you may be children of your Father in heaven; for he makes his sun rise on the evil and on the good, and sends rain on the righteous and on the unrighteous. For if you love those who love you, what reward do you have? Do not even the tax collectors do the same? And if you greet only your brothers and sisters, what more are you doing than others? Do not even the Gentiles do the same? Be perfect, therefore, as your heavenly Father is perfect. (Matt. 5:43-48)

Walter Wink tells us that Jesus could not have said, "Be perfect," and that a better translation would be more like Luke 6:36, "Be merciful, just as your Father is merciful," or be compassionate as your Father is compassionate.[7] Wink suggests the ultimate religious question today is "How can we find God in our enemies?"[8] Jesus says we are to love our enemies because God does. The sun and the rain are gifts to our enemies and us. Jesus lives this out in his table fellowship with people branded as the enemies of God. Wink explains how the enemy is essential to our understanding of our shadow side, to the enemy within. Unlike our mothers or even our friends, our enemies will tell us things about ourselves that we need to know, aspects of ourselves we cannot discover any other way.[9]

Our enemies are also human beings created in the image of God who have a history of suffering and oppression. Henry Wadsworth Longfellow notes, "If we could read the secret history of our enemies, we should find in each [person's] life sorrow and suffering enough to disarm all hostility."[10] I find this statement to be true and an indication of why we need to talk with our enemies. Yes, some of those we call "enemy" do want to hurt us. Yet, if we see the enemy as a human being with fears and sorrows, and the enemy as someone from whom we can learn, not only about ourselves, but also about God, our courage increases and our fear decreases.

Willingness to Risk

Let us be honest. This journey of conflict transformation, especially the decision to love an enemy, involves willingness to risk. Relationships always entail vulnerability. Commitment to relationships with God and neighbor involves letting go of the desire to control, including the outcome of your efforts. It takes courage. Some peacebuilders have been assassinated because they threatened "the powers that be." Peacebuilders become the enemies of systems built on power, greed, oppression, and falsehood. Nevertheless, the capacity to risk makes transcendent change possible. The capacity to risk makes shalom possible: God's goal for all creation of right relations and well-being.

Working for conflict transformation is hard work and takes time. Reconciliation is a journey, so we need to be committed to a journey of a lifetime. Most of the time we do not see what we hoped for, and we never know fully how our work has planted seeds or influenced events. Success is not just measured by visible reconciliation. However, the work of conflict transformation is the most exciting and fulfilling work we can do, and working for reconciliation is our calling.

TWO

Discovering a Theology of Conflict Transformation

Allow the well to fill.

༄༅

*Open your heart and mind to God's love, drawing you
toward reconciliation and being a reconciler.*

O ur theology is what we believe about God and how we view God's work in our lives and in our world. Does our theology lead us to create a well or build a wall? Does our theology open us to loving, healing, reconciling power? What is the theology of conflict transformation/peacebuilding? What is its worldview? How do we understand the structure of reality within which we work as peacebuilders? Our theology is important because it can guide us toward constructive conflict transformation instead of destructive conflict in the name of religion. Our theology makes a difference. Our worldview—our understanding of reality—makes a difference.

The good news of peacebuilding is at the heart of the gospel.[1] Paul often calls God the "God of peace" (Rom. 15:33; 16:20; 1 Cor. 14:33; 2 Cor. 13:11; Phil. 4:9; 1 Thess. 5:23). At Jesus' birth the angels proclaimed peace on earth (Luke 2:14). Each of the first six beatitudes prepares for and builds to the seventh beatitude: "Blessed are the peacemakers, for they will be called children of God" (Matt. 5:9).[2] In the Beatitudes, the steps are: (1) recognizing one's spiritual poverty and need; (2) mourning, caring deeply, about this lack of relationship with God; (3) being meek or humble in relation to God; (4) being hungry and thirsty for a right relation with God and neighbor; (5) becoming pure in heart, pure in love—taking on the nature of the Father; (6) by becoming peacemakers like the Father, being sons and daughters of the Father. In Acts, Luke sums up the ministry of Jesus as "preaching peace" (Acts 10:36). We will explore other scriptures below, but these identify peacebuilding at the heart of the mission and ministry of Jesus. Peacebuilding is not an extracurricular activity.

A Story: An Overview

Dorotheos of Gaza, a sixth-century teacher, frames and visualizes a theological foundation for conflict transformation and peacebuilding that I find appealing. One day the monks of his monastery came to him saying, "We have had it. We can't worship God in the company of our fellow monks." They used this wonderful phrase to describe their problem. It was each other's "ordinary, irritating presence" that got in the way. Does this sound familiar? We can understand how the monks felt.

Dorotheos responded by asking them "to visualize the world as a great circle whose center is God, and upon whose circumference lie human lives. 'Imagine now,' he asked them, 'that there are straight lines connecting from the outside of the circle all human lives to God at the center. Can't you see that there is no way to move toward God without drawing closer to other people, and no way to approach other people without coming near to God?'"[3]

Dorotheos understood that in order to get close to God, we need to get closer to our fellow human beings; and in order to get closer to our fellow human beings, we need to get closer to God. This is interesting, isn't it? God is all mixed up with human relationships, and human relationships are all mixed up with God. We experience the energy of God, the love of God, in our relationships. We experience the divine in relationships, marriages, in working environments as we engage one another more deeply. Dorotheos says we cannot experience either God or our fellow human beings without moving closer to each at the same time. This teaching is the inspiration for the JustPeace symbol on the next page:

Roberta Bondi, who tells this story in her book *Memories of God*, adds:

> There is something implied in the very shape of his imagined chart, however, that Dorotheos did not draw to the attention of his listeners—that in the movement toward love, whether of God, or of another human being, there is an open space so close to the center of reality, that the human and the divine loves become indistinguishable.[4]

Isn't this where we experience the Incarnation?

Another perspective I would add relates to the fact that each of these human beings connected to the center is unique. Looking at God's creation, we know God loves differences. No two human beings have ever been identical. This means each relationship is unique. We need to respect the different relationships we have with each other and with God.

One way to look at this circle is to see the whole circle as God and the center as the heart of God. In God, whether we recognize it or not, we all move and breathe and have our being (Acts 17:28). We live in God, who is closer than our breath. God is not above or beyond but among, within, and between. God is the connective tissue of life. This vision is deeply incarnational. We are each a part of God's body. At the center, all creation comes together. The heart of God is where all is reconciled and made new. This is where we find our full humanity and our authentic selves. We experience our humanity and the divine most fully when we experience a moment of reconciliation.

Love God, Neighbor, and Self

The vision of Dorotheos expresses the Great Commandment, the sum of the law and the prophets: "'You shall love the Lord your God with all your heart, and with all your soul, and with all your mind.' . . . 'You shall love your neighbor as yourself.' On these two commandments hang all the law and the prophets" (Matt. 22:37, 39-40). Life is about loving God, loving ourselves, and loving our neighbors: all together, ideally, all at the same time. We are told that this is the sum of the law and the prophets. If we could understand this one scripture and live it, we would understand the heart and the depth of all the wisdom in the scriptures. What does it mean? What does it tell us about the created order, about reality? What does it tell us about the work of peacebuilding, which is the heart of the gospel?

Creation is relational. We are interconnected and interdependent. There is an ecology of being of which we are a part. We are created for relationship with God and all creation. We are who we are because of our relationships. We know and feel how important relationships are to us, because there is nothing more painful to us than a strained or broken relationship, except the death of a loved one. Our theological worldview is deeply relational and, for Christians, our relationships are not limited by boundaries of nation-states or tribes, or any other walls. All our boundaries are trumped by our baptism into this relationship with God and neighbor.

John Paul Lederach notes, "At the cutting edge of fields from nuclear physics and biology to systems theory and organizational development, relationships are seen as the central organizing concept of theory and practice."[5] Lynn Margulis and Dorion Sagan theorize that the creation of new forms of life occurs through a symbiotic process, and that cooperation and mutual dependence among all life-forms are the central aspects of evolution. "The view of evolution as chronic bloody competition among individuals and species, a popular distortion of Darwin's notion of 'survival of the fittest,' dissolves before a new view of continual cooperation, strong interaction, and mutual dependence among life forms. Life did not take over the globe by combat, but by networking."[6] Evolution is the movement toward higher levels of cooperation and mutual dependence. From quantum theory we learn that "particles come into form and are observed only as they are in relationship to something else. They do not exist as independent 'things.' . . . These unseen *connections* between what were previously thought to be separate entities are the fundamental ingredient of all creation."[7]

Women theologians have been key in clarifying the relational nature of creation for me. Beverly Harrison, my teacher in seminary, introduced me to a relational theology.[8] Carter Heyward sums up this understanding when she talks about "mutual relation":

> By "relation," I am speaking of the radical connectedness of all reality in which all parts of the whole are mutually interactive. The term "mutual" has a double and simultaneous meaning, both metaphysical and ethical, mystical and moral. . . . The white ash, the cat, and I are mutually related—in life together, interconnected ecologically and economically, politically and spiritually, regardless of whether we notice this. In the second place, our moral work as human creatures is to notice this connectedness.[9]

In his book *I and Thou* Martin Buber sees life as the experience not only of the I-It, but the I-Thou or the I-You. In the I-It relationship, we see the other as an object.

> When I confront a human being as my You and speak the basic word I-You to him, then he is no thing among things nor does he consist of things. . . . The basic word I-You can be spoken only with one's whole being. The concentration and fusion into a whole being can never be accomplished by me, can never be accomplished without me. I require a You to become, becoming I, I say You."[10]

Buber goes on to say:

> Extended, the lines of relationships intersect in the eternal You. Every single You is a glimpse of that. Through every single You the basic word addresses the eternal You. The mediatorship of the You of all beings accounts for the fullness of our relationships to them—and for the lack of fulfillment. The innate You is actualized each time without ever being perfected. It attains perfection solely in the immediate relationship to the You that in accordance with its nature cannot become an It.[11]

Bishop Desmond Tutu has helped the world community understand the relational nature of creation. He says, "My humanity is caught up, is inextricably bound up, in yours. . . . A person is a person through other persons. . . . I am human because I belong. I participate. I share." His understanding is informed by the African concept of *ubuntu* and the Christian concept of the body of Christ. At the heart of *ubuntu* is an understanding that I am "diminished when others are humiliated or diminished, when others are tortured or oppressed, or treated as if they were less than who they are."[12] Paul says in his first letter to the Corinthians, "If one member suffers, all suffer together with it; if one member is honored, all rejoice together with it" (1 Cor. 12:26). If we could only appreciate how we are dehumanized when we dehumanize another, we might change our ways. For me, this is a key to our overcoming racism—and all the other isms.

What does this tell us about the human condition and what we call sin? Sin is acting as if you are not interdependent and not in relationship—acting as if God does not exist—being self-absorbed, self-occupied, not focused on the other and the self in relationship. Sin is the rupture of communion with God and our neighbor, as well as with our own true self. In this anxious world, we are all guilty of this rupture. Violence is the key manifestation of sin or evil, the destruction of communion.

God creates and enables relationships. "In the beginning is the Relation."[13] For Buber, this is another way of saying that in the beginning was God. God is a relational being—the one who creates relationship and enables relationship, the one who creates and sustains "the many." All of creation is related in God. We are all interdependent and interconnected in God.

Created in the image of God, we are to focus on the relational nature of life. This means paying attention to the relationship as much as the players in the relationship. Buber says, "The purpose of relation is the relation itself—touching the You. For as soon as we touch a You, we are touched by a breath of eternal life."[14]

To find oneself, attention must shift from oneself to the neighbor and to God. Here the self in relation comes into focus—the loving self, the compassionate self, the authentic self. This is what I understand is meant by losing oneself to find oneself (see Luke 17:33).

God is love. Here is another way to express this reality: God is the energy that relates us. We have learned to call this energy *love*. "Beloved, let us love one another, because love is from God; everyone who loves is born of God and knows God. Whoever does not love does not know God, for God is love" (1 John 4:7-8). Love is essential both to understanding the nature of God and the life we are called to live. God's love is incarnate in creation. We do experience the Divine in simple acts of love. "No one has ever seen God; if we love one another, God lives in us, and [God's] love is perfected in us" (1 John 4:12).

God's love is most clearly seen, for me, in the life and teaching of Jesus: for example, Jesus weeping with Mary and Martha at the grave of Lazarus, Jesus teaching about the good Samaritan and the father of the prodigal son. The ultimate experience is discovering the Creator of the universe on the cross, fully identifying with us, suffering the violence of the world, and then forgiving us, reconciling with us.

We know that God's love is not a limited commodity. God's love is abundant, more than enough for all of us. Nothing can separate us from the love of God (see Rom. 8:38-39).

God loves differences. We have talked previously about the uniqueness of each human being. There has never been another you. We are told that there have never been two snowflakes alike. There are 250,000 different kinds of leaves. There are 9,000 species of birds. Then there are bugs, a diversity of bugs we cannot imagine. Doesn't it appear that God loves diversity and difference? We are learning that biodiversity is important to us as well as to God—human diversity included.

The Bible typically moves from the universal to the particular. Jonathan Sacks, in his book *The Dignity of Difference,* points out that the first eleven chapters of the Bible center around archetypal figures and universals—"Adam and Eve, Cain and Abel, Noah and the Flood, Babel and its tower." He then shows how God, unlike Plato, moves from the universal to the particular—a covenant with "one man, Abraham, one woman, Sarah, and one people, their descendants." God's response to the attempt to impose a human-made unity on divinely created diversity is seen in the story of the Tower of Babel (Gen. 11:1-9). Before the Tower of Babel, everyone spoke the same language. After God responds to the hubris of humankind, many languages were developed—approximately 6,000 languages today. After the Tower of Babel, the movement is to the particular. Sacks concludes that the proposition at the heart of monotheism is that *"unity creates diversity."*[15]

We do see universals in the Bible, such as the covenant with Noah, but they "exist to create space for cultural and religious difference: the sanctity of human life, the dignity of the human person, and the freedom we need to be true to ourselves while being a blessing to others."[16] There are universal truths and these truths are most fully realized when they recognize and appreciate the particular. Our dignity as persons is rooted in this diversity, in our uniqueness. Sacks concludes, "We will make peace only when we learn that God loves difference and so, at last, must we."[17]

God desires unity. "Then God said, 'Let us make humankind in our image, according to our likeness'" (Gen. 1:26). This belief that we are created in the image of God is shared by all of the Abrahamic faiths—Judaism, Christianity, and Islam. This belief is the deep basis for human rights, grounded in the dignity of being created in the image of God. This is our common heritage binding us all together.

As Christians, we see our various gifts as part of the body of Christ. Each part of the body plays an important role in relation to the whole. Something remarkable happened at Pentecost! Here we experience the final chapter in the story that began with the Tower of Babel. All were filled with the Holy Spirit and, although they all spoke different languages, they understood each other. There was unity in the Spirit (Acts 2). This experience of the Spirit of God is the unifying principle of all life and the recognition of our unity with our fellow human beings.

I recently joined twenty legal professionals—lawyers, law professors, and judges—to develop a new paradigm for the lawyer centered in the love of neighbor. We looked at the relational nature of our work: creating and defining relationships, for example, through contracts and restoring broken relationships. We worked together in Loppiano, a town located south of Florence, Italy. This town is one of thirty created by Focolare, a Catholic lay movement started in 1943 by women who were reading the Bible by candlelight during the bombing of Trent. Led by Chiara Lubich, the Focolare movement has been guided by two decisive moments in the life of Jesus: his priestly prayer for unity (John 17:21), and his cry of abandonment on the cross (Matt. 27:46).

For the Focolare movement, this prayer "that they may all be one" is not only for unity of Christians but also for all creation. Loppiano is a town of less than a thousand people from seventy different nations. Our group included a judge from Indianapolis, who is a Muslim and a follower of Warid D. Mohammed, the son of Elijah Mohammed, who differed with his father and brought African Americans into a traditional Muslim practice and faith. Warid was so impressed by Chiara Lubich that he told his followers that they could also be members of Focolare. My judge friend attended Muslim services but also the meetings of Focolare. While we were in Italy, Chiara died, and we found ourselves surrounding her body in her home. We were Jewish, Christian, Muslim, Buddhist lawyers who were Asian, Hispanic, African American, and Caucasian. As we stood around her body together, we represented and experienced her vision. She worked for unity through mutual love. Chiara said, "One thing is clear in our soul: Unity is what God wants of us. We live only to be one with him, one with each other, and one with everybody. This marvelous vocation ties us to heaven and binds us to the one human family."[18]

For Chiara and the Focolare, this search is animated and guided by seeing the face and heart of Jesus forsaken in the lives of each human being. This vision puts us in solidarity with the greatest suffering and pain Jesus experienced and that humanity experiences—feeling abandoned by God. "My God, my God, why have you forsaken me?" (Matt. 27:46). In that cry, the incarnate God most fully identifies with our human condition: alienation from God and neighbor. Here is the common ground for our unity, for the deepest love for God, Jesus, and humanity. Such common ground is the foundation for the faith and motivation to reach out to our neighbors, especially our enemies, and be about the work of reconciliation. What is the result? I had the opportunity to meet at Chiara's home the women, now in their eighties, who started this movement. What I saw in their faces was the joy we have been promised.

God Reconciles and Calls Us to Be Reconcilers

We know we should love God, neighbor, and self, but how can we experience the spirit and the power to do so? Paul tells us:

> So if anyone is in Christ, there is a new creation: everything old has passed away; see, everything has become new! All this is from God, who reconciled us to himself through Christ, and has given us the ministry of reconciliation; that is, in Christ God was reconciling the world to himself, not counting their trespasses against them, and entrusting the message of reconciliation to us. (2 Cor. 5:17-19)

God reconciles. The human world in its self-centeredness is separated from God. In our human relations we are torn apart by violence, hatred, retribution, and apathy. How do we restore the relationship with God and with our neighbors? The answer is we cannot—alone! Only the Love that created and connects us has the ultimate power to reconnect us.

On the cross we see it all come together—the violence, the response to Jesus by the principalities and the powers, and the experience in the midst of the violence of feeling abandoned by God and neighbor. On the cross we see that this is not just the experience of a human being but of God as well, who shares our experience. Here we see that human violence not only affects God's relational world, but is an attack on God's relational being. The good news is God and the relationship cannot be destroyed. Love is stronger than violence and death, and the way of God, which is the only way out of the cycles of violence and retribution, is the way of forgiveness and love.

In this relational world of difference, God's love is at work for right relations and a culture of *justpeace*. God's goal for all creation is shalom—well-being and right relations—with God, with neighbor, and with oneself. This is experienced in the reconciling acts of God. In Jesus, we see God is present in our world, suffers with all creation on the cross, and breaks the grip of the principalities and powers through the word of forgiveness on the cross. In the resurrection, we find victory over death and a new creation. Receiving this power-filled gift, we can do likewise, experiencing the spirit and the energy to reconcile with the neighbor as well as ourselves.

We are called to be reconcilers. God's reconciliation not only empowers us to do likewise but also mandates we participate in a "ministry of reconciliation." Jesus tells us in the Gospel of Matthew that if we are estranged from someone, we are to leave our gift at the altar and be reconciled with the other (Matt. 5:23). Reconciliation is an act of developing a new relationship that is just and right. This process is more important to God than praise and worship. In Amos we read, "Take away from me the noise of your songs; I will not listen to the melody of your harps. But let justice roll down like waters, and righteousness like an ever-flowing stream" (5:23-24).

The reconciler is called to stand in the gaps, often tragic gaps, and help the sides understand each other. As reconcilers, we see the gap between what is and what could or should be in the relationship, between reality and possibility. We live in the tension, assisting parties to see a life-giving way. Living in the tension, we never succumb to only seeing what is, becoming cynical, nor do we just see pure possibility separated from reality and become irrelevant idealists.

Reconciliation is not a hasty process, proclaiming peace where there is no peace, ignoring injustice and human suffering. Reconciliation is intimately connected with justice, with right relations. As Christians, we must restore the work of reconciliation from the periphery to the center of the life and witness of the church where it belongs. My dream is that every church becomes a neighborhood reconciliation center.

The Journey of Reconciliation and Restorative Justice

How do we do this work? What does the journey of reconciliation look like? In all my reading on forgiveness, reconciliation, conflict transformation, and restorative justice, which is another way of talking about reconciliation, I have found nothing more helpful than the eighteenth chapter of Matthew, a Gospel that is a book of instruction to the early church. Here is where the scripture puts flesh and blood on the bones of the Great Commandment and on our calling to be reconcilers.

Matthew 18 begins and ends with two of the greatest sources of conflict and violence: power and money. The chapter begins with the disciples' question: "Who is the greatest in the kingdom of heaven?" It ends with the issue of the forgiveness of debt. One whose debt is bigger than all the debt of Mesopotamia is forgiven. This debtor then turns on his small debtor, throws him into jail, and suffers the consequences of one forgiven who does not forgive. In between, we are given a brilliant analysis as to why we have destructive conflict and violence—the problems created by trying to be greater than another:

- an understanding that God is present with us in the midst of conflict,
- an understanding of why Jesus calls us to be "like a child," or what it means to say peacemakers are children of God,
- practical advice on how to deal with conflict and harm: the journey of reconciliation, the journey of restorative justice,
- the story of the lost sheep with its vision of no one being lost, and the celebration that occurs when restoration of relationship takes place,
- the radical breaking of cycles of woundedness, retribution, and violence through the act of forgiveness, and
- an understanding of the deep reality of creation, seeing the consequence of not following the path of reconciliation and restorative justice, being told that if we do not forgive we will not be able to experience forgiveness, and if we do not follow the journey of responding to those we have harmed, we will not be able to experience the kingdom.

Experiencing God in the Midst of Conflict. In the middle of Matthew 18 is the verse we explored in chapter 1: "For where two or three are gathered [in conflict] in my name, I am there among them" (Matt. 18:20). No one takes the journey of reconciliaton alone. God heals, God restores, and God saves. The only question we have is whether we really believe this. As I have said earlier, the more I work with conflict, the more I am aware that this is where I find God most fully present. The schema below presents the text as a whole.

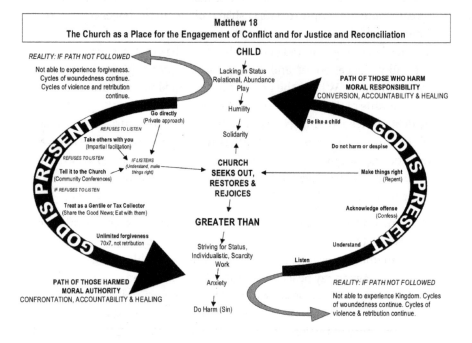

Seeking Out the Lost, Restoring Them, and Celebrating. The heart and soul of this chapter—its Rosetta stone—is the parable of the shepherd in search of the lost sheep.

> What do you think? If a shepherd has a hundred sheep, and one of them has gone astray, does he not leave the ninety-nine on the mountains and go in search of the one that went astray? . . . So it is not the will of your Father in heaven that one of these little ones should be lost. (See Matt. 18:12-14.)

Here we see the understanding of *ubuntu* or shalom elevated to a new level. In this relational world, God desires that no one be lost, whether lost because of causing harm or because of being harmed.

Today we worry about keeping what we have, or not losing more than we have been losing; we live out of a theology of scarcity. We want to make sure we keep the ninety-nine and not lose any of them while we go off looking for the one who is missing. What if we experienced ourselves as the beloved community, or body of Christ, as Paul did, understanding that when the toe is hurting, the whole body hurts?

Aren't we all served when the shepherd seeks out the one who is lost? Moreover, aren't we all shepherds? What if the ninety-nine all seek out the lost together? The health of the community is determined by how the least and the lost are treated. This is not only about individual but also communal healing and reconciliation. What blesses one blesses all. All work together for the good of the whole.

Becoming a Reconciler/Peacemaker: Being Like a Child

In Matthew 18 we hear Jesus describe the type of person we need to be to enter the kingdom. In essence he explains what it means to be a peace-builder. Jesus says, "Truly I tell you, unless you change and become like children, you will never enter the kingdom of heaven. Whoever becomes humble like this child is the greatest in the kingdom of heaven" (Matt. 18:3-4). Chapter 4 deals extensively with what it means to be "like a child." There we will consider the character, the role, and the virtues of the peacebuilder.

Practical Path of Those Harmed. After telling the parable of the lost sheep, Jesus outlines the journey of being restored to community for both the person who is harmed and the one doing the harm, to the child who has been harmed and to the one seeking to be the greatest.

As we go down the path of those harmed and the path of the one who harms, we recognize we have been on both paths ourselves, often simultaneously, experiencing harm and doing harm. Recognizing this, being able to name the fact that all parties have experienced harm, often frees parties in conflict to move forward together. As a party to the conflict, admitting to the other your role in the harm and/or your recognition that the other has been harmed as well is significant in opening up a healing process.

Jesus starts with the path of the person harmed, as the restorative justice process begins with victims and their harm. The person harmed has priority. Jesus describes the victim going to the offender. He is saying that the victims have the moral agency or authority; that they should be empowered to confront and to hold accountable the one who has done harm. The person harmed is the primary moral agent for transformation. The victim is not powerless. For Jesus, this is a way to healing.

As you will see in the following steps, this confrontation is not about revenge but about restitution, amends, making things right. This path is not a path of punishment but a path of accountability and restoration. This is a demanding process. What is the process for dealing with "sin"—with the harm created by another?

1. Go directly to the one who has harmed you. "If another member of the church sins against you, go and point out the fault when the two of you are alone. If the member listens to you, you have regained that one" (Matt. 18:15). Eugene Peterson expresses it this way: "work it out between the two of you" (THE MESSAGE).

Is this the way we usually respond to harm in the church or in the world? When we are harmed or feel harmed, do we not usually avoid speaking directly to the person who harmed us? Instead, we speak to as many other people as possible. We want them on our side. Now with electronic communication, we can send an e-mail to everyone in the world except the person with whom we need to talk. We have all been on the receiving end of these calls and e-mails as people want to get us on their side in a dispute. This problem is especially acute for leaders. The ideal is to get the bishop or the pastor on your side. This is called "triangulation." People want to make their problems your problem.

As leaders and friends, your first question to the person who is trying to triangulate you into their problem is: have you spoken to the other person directly? If they have not gone directly, your role is to encourage them to do so. If the response is that I do not know how to do this, then your role can be to help coach them in the attitudes, skills, and processes that are described in this book. Your role is not to go with them, unless there is an issue of safety or significant imbalance of power, such as a child confronting an adult offender.

"If the member listens to you, you have regained that one" or in *The Message,* "If he listens, you've made a friend" (Matt 18:15). You see here the connection with the shepherd and the lost sheep. What does it mean to listen and to be heard? What does it mean to be heard in a way that leads to regaining the brother or the sister, with being reconciled? Listening is the key to all conflict transformation and a key spiritual practice.

Listening, which will be addressed in greater depth in chapter 3, involves more than the simple act of hearing and understanding what is being said to you. In the Bible, listening also means responding to what you have heard by attempting to address the harm you have created. Responding by making things right is the sure sign that you have listened, heard, and understood.

Listening is encouraged by the way we speak our truth in love. If we simply practiced going directly at an early stage of a conflict, most conflicts would be resolved. But some people are hard of hearing. You have experienced this. Jesus recognizes this and has a second suggestion.

2. Bring witnesses or third parties with you. "But if you are not listened to, take one or two others along with you, so that every word may be confirmed by the evidence of two or three witnesses" (Matt. 18:16). Here, Jesus suggests that the presence of others can help people listen (see Deut. 19:15 and 1 Tim 5:19). How can the witnesses or third parties help? Peterson's contemporary version suggests one answer: "If he won't listen, take one or two others along so that the presence of witnesses will keep things honest, and try again" (THE MESSAGE). These witnesses are not witnesses for one side or the other. They are present to assist both parties in the listening and hearing, so it is honest and productive. In practicing mediation, I am always amazed at how helpful a third party can be to two people in conflict. The third party provides a safe space where people feel empowered to tell their stories as well as to listen to the other's story. The third party can help people move from their position to their needs and interests, getting everyone on the same side of the table working to address each other's needs and interests. Good things happen. Mediation works in a significant percentage of cases. However, Jesus recognizes that sometimes the assistance of one or two others does not result in the necessary listening and response, so Jesus suggests a third way.

3. Tell it to the church. "If the member refuses to listen to them, tell it to the church" (Matt. 18:17). What does this mean? Remembering that this is a process informed by the parable of the lost sheep, we see the church members as advocates for good listening, hearing, accountability, and healing: restoration to the community. Ideally, I imagine the church as a circle of healing and accountability. If the church "takes sides" or makes a premature judgment, the process will break down. Ultimately, the church might be called on to make a decision if the parties themselves cannot agree, including recognizing the decisions of those who have by their actions excluded themselves from community. Such decisions are recognized in heaven (see Matt. 18:18-19).

These decisions regarding life in community are seen as critically important and are sacred decisions with power. These decisions are affirmed by God. Here we see the importance of community and actions that restore community.

Even with the church trying to assist, Jesus recognizes that sometimes this attempt fails as well, as the person does not listen. So Jesus makes a further suggestion.

4. *Treat as Gentiles and tax collectors.* "If the offender refuses to listen even to the church, let such a one be to you as a Gentile and a tax collector," or, as stated by Peterson, "If he won't listen to the church, you'll have to start over from scratch, confront him with the need for repentance, and offer again God's forgiving love" (Matt. 18:17, THE MESSAGE). At times, the church has read this as support for excommunicating or excluding the one who fails to listen. Peterson's paraphrase recognizes that one who does not listen is not being excommunicated by the church. She has excommunicated herself and is still in need of repentance. This translation is consistent with the way Jesus treated Gentiles and tax collectors. Jesus ate with them and spent significant time in their company. It is also consistent with what Jesus tells Peter about forgiveness. Since the person has excommunicated herself by her failure to listen, you might decide, as a leader, that you do not need to spend significant amounts of your time and energy trying to get her to listen. However, to follow Jesus, periodically you might want to try to have lunch where you can again offer God's forgiving love and help her understand the need to be reconciled and restored into the community of the body.

5. *Practice unlimited forgiveness.* "Then Peter came and said to him, 'Lord, if another member of the church sins against me, how often should I forgive? As many as seven times?' Jesus said to him, 'Not seven times, but, I tell you, seventy-seven times'" (Matt 18:21-22). Peter thinks he is being generous. The Hebrew Bible and rabbinic teaching (based on Amos 1 and 2 where the Lord forgives "three transgressions") say forgive three times. Isn't seven times greater? But Jesus is saying to Peter: You don't get it; seventy-seven times. In other words, forgiveness should be unlimited. Here we see the movement of the Bible from Lamech's vengeful "seventy-sevenfold" (Gen. 4:24) to the unlimited forgiveness Jesus calls for.

6. Know the reality of not forgiving. If you do not forgive, you are not able to experience forgiveness. Jesus then tells the parable of the debtor who is forgiven a great debt, but who refuses to forgive the person who owes him a small amount of money.

> Then his lord summoned him and said to him, "You wicked slave! I forgave you all that debt because you pleaded with me. Should you not have had mercy on your fellow slave, as I had mercy on you?" And in anger his lord handed him over to be tortured until he would pay his entire debt. (Matt. 18:32-34)

Jesus goes on to say, "So my heavenly Father will also do to every one of you, if you do not forgive your brother or sister from your heart" (Matt. 18:35).

Does this jar you? What does this mean? First of all, it means that not forgiving has consequences. This is serious business. In the Lord's Prayer, we ask to be forgiven as we forgive our debts or trespasses. Our forgiving is critical to our ability to receive forgiveness. We know we were forgiven before we are asked to forgive and God's mercy and forgiveness is always open to us. However, when we close our heart to forgive another, we close our heart to receiving the forgiveness offered to us.

This is not to say we are coerced to forgive. This is not cheap grace and cannot be manipulated. Forgiveness is always a gift from one person to another, which is primarily a gift to oneself, freeing oneself from the thrall of the offense. The journey to forgiveness does not have a script. Each person who is harmed must pursue this journey at her or his own pace. The person harmed, the victim, sets the agenda.

However, we hear in this scripture a word similar to that of Bishop Tutu in the title of his book *No Future without Forgiveness.* Jesus has taught us that the only way out of the cycles of woundedness, retribution, and violence is through forgiveness.

Path of the One Who Harms. The path of the offender is the path of moral accountability or responsibility. It involves conversion, or *metanoia.* This path is a way to healing and restoration. We will go through the next stages more quickly as we have touched on all this. This is the offender's response to the person harmed.

1. Listen to what the person harmed has to say.
2. Understand what harm you have created.

3. Acknowledge (confess) that you understand the harm you have created.

4. Repent for this harm by trying to make things right. This is about real accountability. In the beginning the person harmed might want your eye or your hand, but what they ultimately need is real accountability, your doing those things through restitution and restoration that work toward making things right, toward healing. An example is the man who testified before the Truth and Reconciliation Commission in South Africa. He confessed his role in destroying a village but said he would spend the rest of his life helping to rebuild it.

5. Pursue healing and restoration. There is nothing retributive about this journey. This is not a punishment system but one of real accountability, a critical requirement for restoring the offender to community.

6. Do not harm. Here Jesus tells us not to repeat harmful conduct. We are to be a new creation, no longer doing those things that destroy neighborliness, like abuse and exploitation.

7. Be like a child (as will be further described in chapter 4).

8. Know the reality of not following this path. If you do not follow this path, you will not enter the kingdom of God. "Truly, I say to you, unless you change and become like children, you will never enter the kingdom of heaven," or in the words of *The Message*: "I'm telling you, once and for all, that unless you return to square one and start over like children, you're not even going to get a look at the kingdom, let alone get in" (Matt. 18:3). Again, this is serious business. How serious? "But if you give them [children] a hard time, bullying or taking advantage of their simple trust, you'll soon wish you hadn't. You'd be better off dropped in the middle of the lake with a millstone around your neck. Doom to the world for giving these God-believing children a hard time! Hard times are inevitable, but you don't have to make it worse—and it's doomsday to you if you do" (Matt. 18:6-7, THE MESSAGE).

The door to the kingdom is always open. Jesus is still ready to eat with you. The reality is that you cannot see the door, or the table, if you are not willing to follow the journey described above.

According to Matthew 18:7-9, we need to cut out that portion of our lives that is getting in the way of our experiencing the kingdom, whether it is idolatry involving money, sex, or possessions: whatever distracts you from the love of God and neighbor. As an exercise by yourself or with a group, write down what you feel you need to cut out of your life, put the paper in an envelope, and periodically open the envelope to evaluate how you are doing.

Unless we follow this journey of conversion, the cycles of woundedness, retribution, and violence continue. We live in a retributive, punishing world, but we are asked by Jesus to follow another way. In Matthew 18 we find an alternative journey to that of retributive justice. We are called to the way of restorative justice. The journey of restorative justice, the subject of chapter 9, is the journey of reconciliation. This is the journey of those who gather at the Table of Holy Communion, a table of reconciliation and restorative justice. In chapter 10 we will examine the role of the Table in the work of building a culture of *justpeace*.

Holiness Is Relational Engagement

Walter Brueggemann summarizes much of what the Bible teaches in his essay "Vision for a New Church and a New Century." He notes that holiness is central to who God is and to our identity. He then documents the movement in the Bible from holiness as separation (purity) to holiness as relational engagement, "the capacity to *be with* and *be for* [others] in ways that heal."[19] This is living out of God's abundant love, not living out of scarcity or anxiety. This is experiencing the generative power of forgiveness. Through relational engagement everything can be reconciled and become new.

For Jesus, what defiles comes from within (Mark 7:20-23). Defilements are distortions of neighborliness: greed and self-indulgence (Matt. 23:23-26). Peter perceives this truth as he struggles with the place of Cornelius, the Gentile, in the covenant and experiences the trance in which he sees and hears God say, "What God has made clean, you must not call profane" (Acts 10:15). Holiness as purity recognizes the truth that we must be different from the culture of the world. We must be peculiar, but what Jesus taught us is that our peculiarity is enacted by relational engagement. This different way of being sets followers of Jesus apart in a world of violence and exclusion.

In Ephesians 4:17–5:2, we see impurity comes from licentiousness and greed—the disruption of social relations. The new ethic is to speak truth; manage anger; share and talk in ways that build up; be kind, tenderhearted, and forgiving. In Colossians 3:5-11 the new ethic is about "simple, obvious, daily practices of respect and enhancement" toward the other,[20] against abuse and exploitation in matters of sex and money. "Above all, clothe yourselves with love, which binds everything together in perfect harmony" (Col. 3:14).

This theology empowers and guides the analysis and discussion throughout this book. Theology matters, but we also need skills for living out this theology. We turn in the next chapter to critical skills and spiritual practices we each need to develop in order to be ministers of reconciliation.

THREE

Learning Relational Skills

Be well prepared.

∽◎◌

Be prepared to listen for understanding,
speak the truth in love, use your imagination,
and practice forgiveness.

Conflict transformation and peacebuilding ("holiness as rela-tional engagement") require skills. In starting the Mennonite Conciliation Service, Ron Kraybill learned from two United Methodists, James Laue and John Adams, that it was not enough to enter a conflict situation with only a theology of peace and a desire to bring peace. Skills are needed.

There are many skills we can learn, but foremost among these are the skills of listening for understanding, speaking the truth in love, using our imagination, and being forgiving. Process skills are described in Part II. All these skills should be seen in the context of how we are going to have good conversations with one another and how we are going to renew the conversation when dialogue breaks down. These skills come together in a conversation that is transformative and healing. For such a conversation to take place we need to listen for understanding, speak the truth in love, and use our imagination. Where harm has been done, the conversation and the relationship cannot be restored without forgiveness.

In the sacred space of conflict, these four skills become spiritual practices, taking us deeper into holiness as relational engagement. They involve a lifetime of learning and practice. I am reminded of my own need to continue to work on my own skills, for example, when one of my children says, "Earth to Dad." In other words, Dad, you are not present and listening. These skills are always formed, informed, and guided by a love that is compassionate, kind, humble, meek, patient, forgiving, and grateful (see Col. 3:12-15). All are informed by our theology and our openness to God through prayer, meditation, and study—both privately and corporately.

Listen for Understanding

"Let everyone be quick to listen, slow to speak, slow to anger" (Jas. 1:19). In *Life Together*, Dietrich Bonhoeffer wrote, "Many people are looking for an ear that will listen. They do not find it among Christians, because these Christians are talking where they should be listening."[1] Listening is an art, a spiritual practice. When doing collaborative work around conflict, this is a critical skill. Elise Boulding, the imminent Quaker peacebuilder, said to me, "All of peacebuilding can be summed up in listening." Conflict transformation is built on this particular skill.

How can you be more effective as a listener? Begin with your own experience. You already know a lot about listening, both bad and good listening. Think for a minute about a time when you experienced bad listening. Perhaps a situation when you needed to speak to someone, and thought you had found a sympathetic shoulder, only to walk away feeling more frustrated than you were in the beginning? Think also of a time when you did a poor job of listening. What have you found detrimental to good listening? Make your own list.

Now reflect on moments when you felt truly heard. What did the listener do to make you feel heard? What do you think of as good listening skills? Again make your own list.

Why is listening so important? Listening speaks to one of our deepest needs, to be understood or feel understood. Yes, we might like people to agree with us, take our side, but it is a great gift when we feel that the person understands us, even if the person does not agree with us. It shows the person cares. It develops trust. It connects us.

Listening acknowledges and honors the other's uniqueness with his or her own stories and truths. We each need to tell our story, and we each need to hear the other's story. Being listened to provides the opening we need to tell our stories, to express feelings and ideas we would otherwise be afraid to voice. In many ways the greatest gift of listening is that it enables us to go deeper into our own stories. Often I don't know what I think until I hear what I say. Elise Boulding talks about prophetic listening, "listening to others in such a way that we draw out of them the seeds of their own highest understanding, their own obedience, their own vision—seeds that they themselves may not have known were there."[2] This form of listening is prophetic in that it guides us to ever deeper levels, so we can begin to see ourselves as God created us and discover more fully our authentic and truest selves. Listening, which includes asking questions, can lead the other person to greater understanding and clarity about themselves.

Listening is important to the person speaking, but it is also important to the listener. In his famous essay on listening, Carl Rogers, a psychologist and communication theorist, says there is a personal "enjoyment when I can really *hear* someone."[3] Listening creates the possibility of learning and being changed, enriching our lives. If we do not listen, our creativity, flexibility, and ability to grow and learn is diminished, our universe is diminished. Through listening, we can understand how we have harmed another, and also how we can make things right. Hearing has consequences, and these consequences can be redemptive.

Believing that we experience God in the flesh, incarnate in life, we can acknowledge that God speaks to us through the other. We, therefore, need to listen for God's voice in the other, who is created in the image of God. John Paul Lederach, a practitioner and teacher of conflict transformation at the University of Notre Dame, says, "Our capacity to listen to God is only as great as our capacity to listen to each other when we are in conflict."[4] We also need to listen to our inner voice, instincts, and intuitions. The Spirit comes to us through our own voice as well. We must learn to trust our own instincts.

Listening to our holy texts and traditions in new ways will yield benefits also. Jonathan Sacks notes, "One of the paradoxes of Judaism is that, though it is a religion of commands (*mitzvot*), biblical Hebrew contains no word that means 'to obey.' Instead it uses the word *shema*, which means to hear, to understand and to respond—to *listen* in the fullest range of senses." Sacks says:

I believe that God is summoning us to a new act of listening, going back to the sources of our faith and hearing in them something we missed before, because we did not face these challenges, this configuration of dilemmas before. . . . God's word is for all time, but our act of listening is of *this* time.[5]

Finally, listening creates the opportunity for the experience of Pentecost, the creation of community in the midst of difference. At Pentecost, everyone spoke different languages, but everyone, as they listened, understood what was being said (Acts 2:5-11).

Listening Involves the Ears, Eyes, and Heart

The single Chinese character for the verb *to listen* includes symbols for ears, eyes, and heart.

Ears are for hearing. We were given two ears and one mouth. The ratio is suggestive. We should spend significantly more time listening than talking. We need to use our mouths to let people know they have been heard, summarizing or paraphrasing what we have heard, and asking questions that help the person go deeper and gain greater clarity. When statements are not conducive to dialogue, we can also reframe them, capturing the essence of what was said but in language that is more constructive. We will say more about these skills in the discussion of imagination.

Eyes express attentiveness. Eyes, in our Western culture, communicate whether we are really being attentive and fully present. In other cultures, looking an elder directly in the eye is a sign of disrespect. In Kenya, for example, looking into the eyes of anyone senior in age is seen as aggressive and dishonoring. Attentiveness is shown more by the welcoming tone of voice. In all our cultures, we need to create a space for the other where they receive our undivided, respectful attention, in ways that are culturally sensitive. If we cannot give this attention, we need to set a time when we can. The whole body can express this attentiveness and openness to the other. Body language is the most important way that we communicate.

The heart expresses empathy. To listen to someone with the heart is to listen with empathy and with care to them and their stories. The heart of good listening is authenticity, genuine curiosity and caring. No matter how good our technique is the other person will know if we do not really care about what they are saying. Listening is not about judging, diagnosing, appraising, or evaluating. Job's friends were very helpful when they just sat and listened and grieved with Job. When these "friends" started judging and diagnosing, they lost their ability to help. Listening with the heart is also about hearing the feelings and emotions that lie beneath the words.

Listening Practices

Listening is clearly fundamental to conflict transformation. It is rooted in our deepest moral inclinations. What, then, are the practices that help bring it about?

Create the space for listening. We first need to create the space for being attentive, mentally and physically, to what the other has to say. The mental space is the most important—a space within ourselves, a space that is open and receptive and caring. This involves prayerful preparation if the conversation is a difficult one. When time does not allow for this preparation, we can suggest a time when we are able to be mentally and physically present. The most important part of the physical space is what we create with our own presence and body language, including an open posture and a welcoming tone of voice. For us in the West, this involves eye contact, and an open and receptive posture. We know what it is like to speak to someone who will not look you in the eye and whose arms are crossed. The physical space ideally involves a place that is quiet, inviting, and comfortable, with no distractions. For larger conversations, something to drink and eat is helpful in creating the space, as well as a space recognized by all as neutral ground.

Ask good questions. A good question is open-ended and builds on what has been said; it takes the person deeper into their story. In the early stages of a conversation, these questions might be primarily clarifying questions, questions for understanding. As a conversation progresses, good questions open up more aspects of a person's story, the deeper levels of the story.

These questions are different than a lawyer's questions in cross examination. In cross examination, a lawyer is not interested in the other's story but in getting that person to agree with the story the lawyer wants told. Curiosity is not an element in the questions. In fact, in law school, students are told never to ask a question for which they do not know the answer.

In conflict transformation, we ask questions that grow out of caring for what the other has to say, out of genuine curiosity. An open-ended question can be answered by the person on his or her own terms. Ask questions that connect with what has been said and communicate that you have heard the other person. The question itself might contain a short paraphrase as an introduction to the question. Such questions do not interrupt the story but emerge out of what is being said. We will speak about asking questions in greater depth in chapter 7.

Summarize and paraphrase. Simply summarizing or paraphrasing what you have heard is a good way to make sure you are hearing correctly and to show others they have been heard. Paraphrasing puts what the other person said into your own words. You say what you have heard and ask if you have stated the concern, emotion, or content correctly. Recognize the emotions as well as the words.

Summarizing is generally done by a facilitator to bring together what a variety of people have said. This is all part of a conversation, so the summary or paraphrase should be brief.

In good conversation—dialogue—good listening and speaking come together. Let us turn now to the role of the speaker and the significance of speech.

Speak the Truth in Love

"Speaking the truth in love, we must grow up in every way into him who is the head, into Christ" (Eph. 4:15). God speaks and there is light (Gen. 1:3). Speaking can create. Speaking can make sense and give meaning to our reality. Through speaking we can also hurt and destroy.

One lesson I learned in South Africa was the power in telling and hearing stories. We saw the power of being able to tell stories in a safe place where there is true listening, especially after experiencing the suppression or denial of a story. We have learned from working with trauma that in order to move beyond the grip of grief, anger, and trauma we need to tell our truth as we have experienced it. These stories are our truth and they need to be told and they need to be heard. Being open to the truth of the story, the truth found in the other's story is a different exercise than establishing the facts. Truth is more than the facts of what happened. Truth includes the emotional impact of the events. A single-minded focus on establishing the facts can get in the way of seeing the truth in the story, because it creates an adversarial relation and misses the deeper truths as well as any hope of reconciliation.

I am also convinced that nothing is more powerful in changing our views and opinions than hearing the personal story of another. Sacks says, "We must learn the art of conversation, from which truth emerges not, as in Socratic dialogues, by the refutation of falsehood but from the quite different process of letting our world be enlarged by the presence of others who think, act, and interpret reality in ways radically different from our own."[6] In difficult conversation, such as around homosexuality, stories move people and enlarge their world. In every person's story there is sorrow and suffering. We need to provide places where we can hear and understand the journey of the other and the other's suffering, particularly our enemies. There is nothing more important we can do for peace than to talk with our enemies and hear their stories.

Speaking Practices

Telling our own story is not easy, because it demands self-revelation, vulnerability, and self-knowledge. Moreover, it makes a difference how you tell your story. Think about the type of speech that closes off communication and shuts you down, or even makes you angry and willing to fight. Write down the characteristics of such speech.

Think for a moment about this statement, as if it were directed at you: "You are a spiteful person, and everyone says so." What is wrong with this statement? First of all, it is focused on your character, your very being. How do you respond to such a statement? Such a generalization does not refer to something specific, to which you could respond. It represents the thoughts of people not in the room who are not part of the conversation. How do you respond to everyone? What are some of the practices of speaking the truth in love?

Focus on giving information about yourself. Give information about your emotions, your needs, and the impact of the situation on you. These are called "I statements." These are different from the "You statements" such as the one above, that judge, blame, mind read, and demand. "You statements" create a defensive response. "I statements" are self-revelatory statements by the speaker and give the listener the opportunity of dealing with the speaker's feelings, responses, and observations, which is very different from defending one's essential being.

For example, "I *feel* [state the feeling] *when you* [state the behavior] *because* [state the effect.]" "I feel hurt when you do not respond to my phone calls because I surmise that you do not care about our relationship." This is much better than saying, "You are rude and uncaring for not responding to my phone calls and cutting off our relationship."

"I statements" help describe what is true for you without blaming. They are rooted in your feelings in response to specific conduct. Your feelings are important and need to be expressed. You can't heal what you can't feel. Speak from your heart.

Be specific; do not talk in generalities. I learned early on from my wife that generalizations about our children's conduct were not helpful. Instead of saying that you are a slob because you left your coat in the middle of the hallway, my wife taught me to address the conduct, the specific act of leaving the coat, not their very being. We often use generalizations to identify groups of people or cultures in ways that cause significant harm. One practical guideline for stopping generalizations is to avoid the words "all," "always," and "everyone."

Speak only for yourself, not for others. We love to speak about our problems with everyone other than the person with whom we have the problem. We like to get everyone on our side. Then we like to tell the other person everyone agrees with us. Matthew 18:15 says that we should speak directly to the person with whom we have a problem. When we do so, we need to speak for ourselves and no one else. The person can then address you. There is no way that the other person can address people who are not in the room. Conflict transformers ask people to share from their own experience. Greater understanding and empathy increases when individuals speak for themselves.

Be brief and to the point. Enough said. You know all too well how you and others have gone on and on. This does not allow for conversation or response. It does not show that you respect the other person's right to speak. People get frustrated with long speeches. One of the key guidelines for any conversation is to be brief and to the point.

Tell your story truthfully and with clarity. Being honest is a key to authenticity and to getting a thoughtful and constructive response. We are all disarmed when we hear someone speaking the truth, especially a truth that expresses the speaker's understanding of his or her own failings or limitations. Honesty walks with humility.

Think about what is important to say in a difficult conversation and make it as clear as possible. This preparation takes time and effort before a conversation begins. Yes, in difficult conversations, it is hard to be clear. We need each other's help in clarifying our own needs and interests, but work on trying to be as clear as possible in your own mind. You will learn much about your needs and interests from your own self-reflection. Journaling or making a list of what we wish to share are simple techniques for clarifying our thoughts.

Tell the truth that heals. What is your goal in telling your story? Is it to punish the other? If it is, the result of this will be the end of the conversation and perhaps the relationship. Is this really what you want, or do you want to be heard in order to find healing? It makes a difference how you tell your story. In chapter 10, we will talk about how Jesus taught us at the Last Supper to name the elephant in the room, "one of you is going to betray me," and then give bread, not a stone or punishment. Naming to give bread, to heal, changes the way you speak the truth. Speaking in this way requires the use of our imagination.

Use Your Imagination

"Do not remember the former things, or consider the things of old. I am about to do a new thing; now it springs forth, do you not perceive it?" (Isa. 43:18-19). Violence is the greatest expression of a lack of imagination. Much of our destructive conflict is due to the failure of our imagination. A high degree of imagination is required of those in our culture who would follow Jesus and love God and neighbor. Sadly, imagination seems to be missing from much of the life of the world, as well as of the church.

Walter Brueggemann suggests, "It is the vocation of the prophet to keep alive the ministry of imagination, to keep on conjuring and proposing futures alternative to the single one the king wants to urge as the only thinkable one."[7] Using our imagination releases our creativity, opens our minds and hearts to the leading of the Holy Spirit, which involves being carried by the Spirit to places and ideas we never dreamed possible. For me, the skill of the imagination is theologically grounded in a creator God, a barrier-breaking Jesus, and the Holy Spirit. Using our imagination is where we can experience our participation as co-creators of God's vision of shalom, where we can experience connections and relations as Jesus did, and where our spirits can soar, experiencing the power and the wonder of Pentecost. This is a redemptive imagination.

Using our imagination involves improvisation, being flexible, and being open to the moment, to the other, and to the deep resources of the Spirit. This requires letting go of our desire to control the outcome or the solution and to go with the Spirit.

Practices of the Imagination

Brainstorming. The technique with which we are most familiar is brainstorming. The most exciting time in any facilitation of a conflicted situation is when the parties have agreed on a list of issues and together begin to brainstorm potential options to address each issue and the needs and concerns of all the parties. We will talk more about brainstorming in the context of a facilitation in chapter 8, but here I want to think about how we prepare ourselves and coach others in the use of brainstorming. Name an issue that is involved in the conflict. Let go of assumptions and positions for a moment and create as many possible ideas and solutions as possible, without censoring any of them. When you have exhausted your imagination, begin to evaluate each idea. In doing this you will prepare yourself or prepare another for brainstorming together with the other side.

Reframing. One of the specific skills of the imagination is reframing a problem or an issue or a conflict in a way that opens up constructive options not seen without the new frame. This is an important skill for facilitators or mediators, a skill which will be further discussed as we deal with how we engage others. This skill is also important as you prepare yourself for dealing with a conflict or coaching others on how to do so.

Do you see the bottle as half full or half empty? This is the same bottle with the same liquid, but two different frames for looking at the bottle. It makes a difference if you see it half full. In a child custody case, it makes a difference how you see the issue. Is it a question of which parent will win or have ownership of the child? What if the issue is reframed as how do we maximize the parent-child relationship and/or do what is best for the child? The reframing provides a new focus. Reframing the issues opens up new possibilities and fresh ways of looking at this situation.

Reframing takes imagination. It starts with understanding the deep interests and values of each party. Reframing moves the language from one of positions, judgments, and biases to more neutral language that states what the interests and needs are. As John Paul Lederach explains, "The moral imagination refuses to frame life's challenges, problems, and issues as dualistic polarities."[8] It works at perceiving the highest aspirations of the parties and building on these.

Over time, the Bible reframes the question of how to respond to harm from others. The Bible starts with the law of Lamech: unlimited retribution or revenge: "If Cain is avenged sevenfold, truly Lamech seventy-sevenfold" (Gen. 4:24). The frame then shifts to limited retribution or proportional retribution, an eye for an eye (Exod. 21:23-25). Finally, Jesus frames the response as unlimited forgiveness. "Then Peter came and said to him, 'Lord, if another member of the church sins against me, how often should I forgive? As many as seven times?' Jesus said to him, 'Not seven times, but, I tell you, seventy-seven times'" (Matt. 18:21-22).

Jesus was the great "reframer." In chapter 10 we will reflect on how Jesus at the Last Supper moved from the frame of naming the harm to give a stone or punishment, to naming the harm to give bread, new life, and right relations.

How can we reframe the fight over music or building a new sanctuary or even abortion and homosexuality? You are right. This is going to require great imagination. We know that the frame, if it is to open us to the reality of God's beloved community, will be formed by love.

See complexity as a friend. Oliver Wendell Holmes Jr., the great jurist, exclaimed, "I would not give a fig for the simplicity this side of complexity, but I'd give my life for the simplicity on the far side of complexity."[9] In his book *The Moral Imagination: The Art and Soul of Building Peace*, John Paul Lederach says that a key to the imagination is seeing "complexity as a friend." Why? First of all, because life is complex and peacebuilding is a complex endeavor. Living well with ambiguity is a sign of maturity. Second, because it generates a sense of humility which is realistic and open to newness. Seeing complexity as a friend helps us envision "new angles, opportunities, and unexpected potentialities that surpass, replace, and break the shackles of historic and current relational patterns of repeated violence."[10] Third, it opens us to appreciate difference and the three approaches which we will describe below: saving the other's proposition, experiencing paradoxical curiosity, and practicing the metaphorical process.

Save the other's proposition. Another specific practice of the imagination is helping the other save his or her proposition in a way that is more constructive and fruitful than expressed before. Father Ray Helmick, a Jesuit priest with whom I teach, has opened up for me one of the key underlying principles of Ignatius in his *Spiritual Exercises.* An introductory page in this manual is called the *"Praesupponendum,"* the "Presupposition" for the exercises. It reads:

> To assure better cooperation between the one who is giving the Exercises and the one who receives them, and more beneficial results to both, it is necessary to suppose that every good Christian is more ready to save the proposition of another than to condemn it as false. If he is unable to save the proposition, the one who made it should be asked how he understands it, and if he understands it badly, it should be discussed with him with love. If this does not suffice, all appropriate means should be used so that, understanding his proposition rightly, he may save it.[11]

Father Ray notes:

This is not simply a proposal of Christian charity in our discourse. It is a theory of knowledge, applicable to all, Christian or not; specific to the Christian only insofar as it is a practical living-out, in its openness to the other, of Christian faith. If I am to win all the arguments, know it all beforehand, my mind has already shut down. The proposition of the other, of course, refers to what is truly important in the other's perception, experience, conviction. It is not as if there were no truth criterion. If I am to learn, I must approach the other's proposition with openness. Winning an argument will get me nowhere and I will lose the light that the other's perception could give me. But the other will learn also, coming to an understanding of his own proposition that will enrich it and lead deeper into truth.[12]

In a difficult conversation between two different propositions, the process is a conversation in which both parties work, not to defeat the other's proposition, but to help each discover the best of his or her proposition and save it. As Father Ray points out, we need to become the guarantor of each other's differences. This takes imagination.

Experience paradoxical curiosity. One of the four disciplines of the moral imagination, according to Lederach, is "the ability to sustain a paradoxical curiosity that embraces complexity without reliance on dualistic polarity." Like Father Ray, he sees the problem of reducing the complexity of life to dualistic polarities, either-or propositions, with the underlying theme being, I am right and you are wrong; I am good and you are evil. We do create polarities to protect ourselves from complexity. "The gift of paradox provides an intriguing capacity: It holds together seemingly contradictory truths in order to locate a greater truth. *Curiosity* suggests attentiveness and continuous inquiry about things and their meaning."[13]

For me, this process is primarily the search for higher ground where we can hold together these competing ideas and energies. Ultimately, it is about breaking down the walls of hostility and about healing. This is the work of the imagination.

Practice the metaphorical process. As an English major I was intrigued by the power of metaphor to open up our ability to see connections not seen before. The metaphorical process involves bringing together things not usually seen together, and seeing connections not seen before. My seminary thesis was on the metaphorical experience of Jesus as the

Christ. What happened when the man Jesus was seen together with the vision of the Christ? A new connection was observed, a new understanding of both Jesus and the Christ was realized, and the most profound revelations we have experienced about God and being human were discovered. When we come together with our differences, we are bringing together images, symbols and values that we are rubbing up against each other. If we are committed to the metaphorical process in the work of conflict, we will be committed to seeing the connections that we had not seen before. For me, the metaphorical process is a way of discovering "unity in diversity," of seeing the "one in the many."

The most important revelation was the revelation that God forgives us. We heard this word from the cross. Let us now turn to the fourth discipline of being forgiving.

Be Forgiving

"Then Peter came and said to him, 'Lord, if another member of the church sins against me, how often should I forgive? As many as seven times?' Jesus said to him, 'Not seven times, but, I tell you, seventy-seven times'" (Matt. 18:21-22). Jesus also says, "For if you forgive others their trespasses, your heavenly Father will also forgive you; but if you do not forgive others, neither will your Father forgive your trespasses" (Matt. 6:14-15).

Stop for a moment and consider all the sermons you have heard on forgiveness. Write down what you have been taught. What have you actually seen and experienced in your life? Think of your own struggles dealing with those who have hurt you. Now write down what you have learned from your observations and firsthand experiences, including any questions about forgiveness that concern you.

Before going to South Africa, I had heard a lot of sermons on forgiveness, but I rarely had seen forgiveness practiced. I confess that I know from my own experience how hard it is to forgive. In South Africa, I learned what can happen when the practice of forgiveness is deep in your bones. I learned this from Nelson Mandela, who asked his jailer to be a guest at his inauguration, but I also learned it from most of the people I met. And what a difference it makes.

In this chapter we can only begin to identify the importance of forgiveness, a sense of what it is and what it is not, and some of the guideposts on the journey of forgiveness. Forgiveness is at the heart of the gospel and is an essential practice. How do we practice it? Chapter 2's discussion of

Matthew 18 put forgiveness in the larger context of restorative justice and reconciliation, which will be amplified in chapter 9. Forgiveness is founded on grace and alive with mystery.

A Story Briefly Told

Walter Everett was the pastor of a United Methodist Church in Connecticut. One night he learned his son had been killed by another resident of his son's apartment house. He experienced all the emotions that one would expect, including deep anger and bitterness. He started going to a meeting of a group of people who had also experienced the death of a loved one through a criminal act. As he attended these meetings he discovered that there were people in the group who had been coming for years, up to twenty years, and they were as angry and bitter as ever. They were tragically impacted by the crime, and now they were dying within themselves. He decided this was not the way his son would want him to live or he wanted to live. He realized this anger was only hurting him and that he needed to be free of the thrall of the offense. Over time he reached out to the young man who killed his son. In the process, he came to forgive the young man. Later, he officiated at the young man's wedding. Together they now speak to groups about forgiveness and restorative justice.

Walter invited me to address the first international meeting of Murder Victims' Families for Reconciliation. I listened to the stories—stories very similar to Walter's. I also looked into the eyes of these mothers and fathers, brothers and sisters, daughters and sons. I saw the pain, but I also saw a joy and peace that I did not expect. In their journey toward forgiveness and reconciliation, they had reached deep places, to the heart of God.

The Importance of Forgiveness

Peter thinks he is being generous. As mentioned in chapter 2, the Hebrew Bible and rabbinic teaching say forgive three times. Isn't seven times greater? But Jesus says to Peter, You don't get it. You should forgive seventy times seven. In other words, forgiveness should be unlimited.

In Matthew 18, Jesus then tells the parable of the debtor who is forgiven a great debt, but who refuses to forgive the person who owes him a small amount of money. We have reflected on this story in chapter 2. What we learned is that if we do not forgive, we will not be able to experience forgiveness. This is not because forgiveness is not being offered by

God, but because we do not have the heart to receive it. Our forgiving is critical to our ability to receive forgiveness. We also have learned that it is critical to breaking the cycles of woundedness, retribution, and violence. In fact, I believe ultimately there is no other way out of these cycles. As Desmond Tutu says, there is "no future without forgiveness."

We should also recognize here the problems we create for ourselves when we do not enter the journey to forgive. You can get stuck in the anger and the bitterness. Father Michael Lapsley, a victim in South Africa of a letter bomb sent to him in a church publication, says,

> If something terrible has happened to you, to those you love, it is an understandable and normal response to hate, to be bitter, to want revenge. The problem is . . . it will not destroy our enemies, it will destroy us. We have to find ways of acknowledging the poison and letting it go. That is a journey we need to travel.[14]

As Walter Everett discovered, not undertaking the journey to forgiveness involves a double injury—one imposed from the outside and the second imposed from the inside. We can get stuck in the anger and the bitterness. We do further harm to ourselves as seen, for example, in substance abuse, workaholism, overeating. We experience physical ailments and emotional ailments such as depression, apathy, anxiety, and inability to trust. We often do harm to those close to us through emotional distance and domestic abuse. We also do harm to the one who harmed us and continue the cycles of woundedness, retribution, and violence.

The Elements of Forgiveness

For many, forgiveness is not only impossible but also unjust. Is this because of what they have been taught about forgiveness? Forgiveness is not weakness but an act of great strength. Forgiveness is not denial of the wrongdoing, excusing the wrongdoing, or condoning the wrongdoing. Forgiveness is not giving up on the quest for justice. What do we mean by forgiveness? These are the concepts that have helped me understand and, hopefully, practice forgiveness.

- *Forgiveness is a journey.* There is no one script for everyone. Every journey is different. The journey takes time, and everyone must be patient and follow their own pace. We need to be forgiving of ourselves. We need friends on this journey.

- *Forgiveness is a choice, a decision we make.* Forgiveness cannot be coerced or manipulated. It is an act of the will, a decision made with the whole being—mind, heart, and body.
- *Forgiveness is primarily a gift we give to ourselves.* Forgiveness is the gift of releasing ourselves from the burden of anger, bitterness, and the thrall of the offense. Repressed anger and hatred create emotions that make us sick. We can find this release even if the other person is not alive or available, even as we recognize that it is more effective if we can offer forgiveness to the other. This gift frees us from continuing to feel like a victim. In forgiving, we take control of our own life.
- *Forgiveness is a gift we give the other.* Ideally, forgiveness emerges in response to an apology and a readiness by the offender to make things right. It is, however, not dependent on this. Waiting for the other to do what is right keeps us under the offender's control. In Matthew 18 Jesus talks about the person harmed taking the initiative. Forgiveness is a gift to the other, a gift with the potential of opening the other up to do what is right.
- *Forgiveness breaks us out of the cycles of violence, revenge, and retribution.* In forgiveness we release feelings of ill will and pursue a journey that leads to a different kind of justice, one that is restorative and not retributive, one that includes accountability—an accountability that addresses our needs and has the possibility of healing for all. (This we will pursue further in chapter 9.)
- *Forgiveness is not reconciliation, but it is the only way to reconciliation.* Forgiveness happens in us and by us. Reconciliation is a mutual act and happens in relationship. Forgiveness is about healing one's self. Reconciliation involves healing relationships. Reconciliation does not happen without forgiveness.

The Journey of Forgiveness

The work of Olga Botcharova in dealing with the violence, harm, and trauma of the wars and atrocities within the former Yugoslavia has enabled me to understand the journey of forgiveness. In her visual model opposite, the inner circle represents the journey of retribution and violence.[15] The outer journey is one of healing and reconciliation. Here is a brief summary of four lessons about this journey.

(1) *Finding safety is important to breaking free from the cycle of retribution and violence.* The person harmed should not be harmed again.

From Aggression to Reconciliation

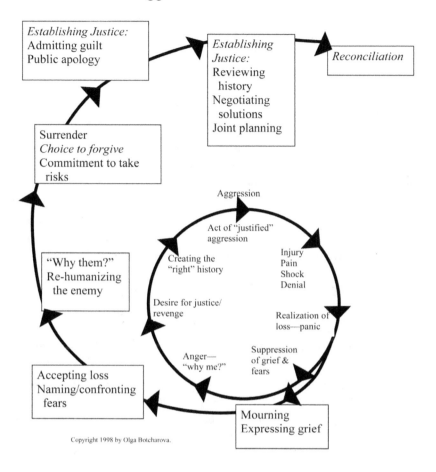

Copyright 1998 by Olga Botcharova.

This involves physical as well as emotional safety. The problem is we are trying to break out of the cycles of violence and retribution, while living in them. If you or your community cannot create such safety, the person harmed must find the type of inner strength that Viktor Frankl found in the midst of a concentration camp, as described in his book *Man's Search for Meaning*.[16] This safety is ultimately found in our God who says, "Do not fear, take courage, for I am with you."

(2) *Mourning, grieving our story, and expressing our fears are essential to our healing and to the integration of the loss into our story.* Forgiveness does not involve denial or suppression of our grief, our fears, and our acknowledgment, with our natural anger, that we have been harmed.

Beverly Harrison taught me about "The Power of Anger in the Work of Love."[17] Our anger says that we take the world and the other seriously. It expresses a natural reaction to injustice. This anger needs to be articulated and acknowledged. We need to name the injustices that have been done to us. We need truth telling. Remaining in a state of anger will not move us forward.

Lamentation plays a valuable role, as seen in the Bible in the book of Lamentations and in the Psalms. Verbalizing our grief and our fears through telling our story, sometimes repeatedly, is necessary. We cannot be silenced. Telling the story with all its emotions to people who listen and care is essential. You cannot heal what you cannot feel. We know the healing journey becomes easier when our story and hurt are acknowledged by the one who harms us, but that may not always be possible. The hope is to integrate the story into our larger narrative as we move toward re-storying our life. The harm cannot be undone. It is a part of our narrative, but over time it can be part of the larger narrative of the journey to forgiveness and even reconciliation.

(3) *Recognizing the other's story is key to rehumanizing the one who harmed you and to moving toward a decision to forgive.* Carolyn Yoder says, "The universal cry, 'Why me?' or 'Why us?' reflects the longing to find reason and meaning in difficult life events. Yet continually asking these often-unanswerable questions keeps us stuck. Together with suppressed fears, these questions provoke the greatest anger at everything and everyone associated with the perpetrator. To restore the ability to think rationally, the question needs to be reframed to 'Why them? Why did they do it, and why did they do it to us?' This opens the way to search for root causes and to acknowledge that the other, the enemy, also has a story."[18]

This reframing is not about condoning what happened, but it does open up the possibility of understanding why we were harmed. The fact is the other has a story, and it is good to know that story. Otherwise, we end up in simplistic, polarizing good-vs.-evil narratives that do not offer a good way to the future together. Life is always more complex than such narratives. The "enemies" are fellow human beings, children of God. In the story of the person who harmed us we find the lessons of interconnections and interdependence. We develop an understanding which allows us to act rationally. It can even yield compassion.

(4) *Choosing to forgive is the act of the will primarily for your benefit, but also for the benefit of the other.* Yes, forgiveness does involve taking a

risk. We are talking about engagement with someone who has done you harm, someone Jesus calls an "enemy." It does involve the willingness to coexist. It best comes in an engagement with the other. In fact, it is often an act of engagement that leads to the decision to forgive, an engagement as suggested in Matthew 18. Ultimately, forgiveness is a decision you control, and only you can make it.

The Craft of Forgiveness

L. Gregory Jones in his book *Embodying Forgiveness* describes forgiveness as a craft that needs to be learned, "embodying . . . forgiveness through specific habits and practices that seek to remember the past truthfully, to repair the brokenness, to heal divisions, and to reconcile and renew relationships."[19] In recent years we saw the ability of the Amish to forgive the person who killed their youth at school. We are told that this happened in an unorganized spontaneous way: individuals began showing up at the home of the parents of the killer, who killed himself as well. Forgiveness is a way of life for the Amish. As in South Africa, the way of forgiveness lies deep in their bones. Like any other skill, we need to spend time working on this craft. We will have plenty of opportunities to practice.

In Conclusion

I am thankful for the spiritual practices of listening, speaking the truth in love, using our imagination, and forgiving. There are other skills to add to your toolbox and to your way of life, but to me these are the most important. Most other skills relate in some way to these skills. Welcome to a lifetime of growth in all these skills, and remember that they are all clothed in love.

FOUR

Becoming Peacebuilders

Be well. Be a well.

∽◎↶

Be a mediating presence in the midst of conflict.

In becoming a peacebuilder, a reconciler, a practitioner of conflict transformation, attitude, theology, and the development of skills or spiritual practices are all important! We also need to be formed by the character and values of the peacebuilder, and we need to understand the role we can and should play. This formation and understanding of role are critical to our own well-being, as we live and work in the midst of conflict. It is also critical to our ability to help others find greater wholeness and well-being or shalom in their relational lives. To understand the role we can and should play, we also need to let go of role expectations that cannot be fulfilled—expectations that lead to unnecessary anxiety and fear, dis-ease, burnout, and potential harm to others.

Peacebuilders as Children of God: Being Like a Child

In the Beatitudes, Jesus associates being a child of God with being a peacemaker. Eugene Peterson helps us understand Jesus' vision in his contemporary wording of Matthew 5:9: "You're blessed when you can show people how to cooperate instead of compete or fight. That's when you discover who you really are, and your place in God's family" (THE MESSAGE). Being a peacemaker means discovering who you really are and what it means to be fully human. For Jesus, this means conversion to being like a child—a child of God.

In Matthew 18 in response to the question by the disciples, "Who is the greatest in the kingdom of heaven?" Jesus answers by putting a child "among them" (Matt. 18:1-2). Jesus says, "Truly I tell you, unless you change and become like children, you will never enter the kingdom of heaven. Whoever becomes humble like this child is the greatest in the kingdom of heaven" (Matt. 18:3-4).[1] In this scripture Jesus turns our world upside down and puts those seeking to be the greatest at the bottom and the child, who was the least in Roman culture, at the top, defining the child as the greatest. What is Jesus trying to tell us through this social reversal? What problems are created by striving to be greater than another, whether in power, money, sex, or goodness, or even humility? In a conflicted and violent world, why should or could human beings, including peacebuilders, be like children?

Jesus' proposition sounds as strange to us as it did to his disciples. I understand Nicodemus's question: "How can anyone be born after having grown old?" (John 3:4) I personally would like to grow up, gain a little maturity, be a wise elder, put away some of my childish things. Why would I want to be like a child? Being like a child as a mature person cannot be a return to naiveté or ignorance of the world. It is not about being childish, as we are also told to put away childish things (1 Cor. 13:11). This image also troubles people who have been treated like a child rather than with the respect they deserve. I am also aware that childhood is complex and that we have positive and negative experiences with children.

Recently I have begun to connect this calling to be like a child with a vision of the peacemaker as the child of God. Struggling with the strangeness of this proposition, I have come to appreciate the reality, the maturity, and the wisdom of the conversion to be "like a child" that Jesus seeks in all of us, including peacebuilders. We can learn what it means to be a peacemaker by understanding what it means to be like a child.

Let Go of Striving for Status or Control

A child in Roman society was simply property, with no rights. Slaves had more rights than children. So the first thing Jesus communicates is that the life to which he calls us is not about striving for status. In fact, it is about being in solidarity with those with no status. For Jesus, the child is representative of the widow, the orphan, the alien. Jesus says, "Whoever welcomes one such child in my name welcomes me" (Matt. 18:5). To "welcome a child," to be in solidarity with the least, is to receive Jesus himself.

Jesus does not mean we should not appreciate our own greatness, the abundant gifts and resources with which we're blessed. The problem for Jesus is our striving to be greater than another, living out of scarcity—not enough power, love, or resources. It is a life of comparison, anxious expectations, and the need to prove oneself, instead of simply being authentically yourself, letting your song be sung, your calling lived fully. Trying to be greater than another leads not only to a lack of neighborliness but also to idolatry—worship of money and power, for example. For Jesus, trying to be greater is the problem of the "Domination System," described by Walter Wink, a system "characterized by unjust economic relations, oppressive political relations, biased race relations, patriarchal gender relations, hierarchical power relations, and the use of violence to maintain them all."[2]

Isn't the message clear that, for Jesus, peacemakers, children of God, are those who do not seek status for themselves and who live in solidarity with all God's creation, particularly the least? A good mediator gives all the credit for any success to the participants. Not seeking recognition or praise is key to being able to empower others to find their voice, to solve their own problems, and to leave the mediation believing they can continue to be constructive in transforming their future conflicts. At the end of any facilitation, the first thing I do is congratulate the parties on their good work. When they say, "It would not have happened without your help," I immediately reply, "You deserve all the credit. It would not have happened without your courage, commitment to the process, and good work."

Seeking status and seeking control go together in our anxious and fearful lives. One of the most important epiphanies I have experienced happened on an airplane to South Africa in 1996. You probably do not know this, but lawyers can be very controlling. While on the long flight overseas, I had a vision of myself as a sailor in a sailboat with the sail closely hauled, going up against the wind, and with my hand firmly gripping the tiller, directing the boat in the direction I wanted it to go. I was in control. I then began to look at my life as a trial lawyer. I controlled or thought I controlled a courtroom; as a managing partner of a law firm, I thought I had some control of the law firm. There were times when my family thought I was controlling. What followed next was the sensation of letting out the sail, going with the wind or the Spirit, and loosening my grip on the tiller to a very light touch. I can remember feeling my whole body relax and the rush that came with the feeling that I was going with the wind, with the Spirit. This letting go of striving to control was one of the most significant moments in my life. I still make lists, and I still have a grip, although generally looser, on the tiller, but my primary goal and experience is letting go and going with the Spirit. And the Spirit has taken me, first in South Africa, and ever since, to places much better and more interesting than any place I was striving to steer my boat. I have found myself and my own well-being when I have allowed the Spirit to lead me. I have been, in my better moments, led into a life abundant at the "pace of guidance," as Ron Kraybill describes it.[3]

This has become a guiding image for me as a mediator, facilitator, peacebuilder. As a facilitator, I consciously let go of any desire to control the outcome. I may envision some avenues the parties might develop based on my analysis and my preparation with the participants. However, as I enter the room with the parties, I consciously let go of any agenda I might have for the result. I verbally affirm in the beginning that the group has the wisdom to deal with whatever they are facing. In fact, I state that I am not a magician or a miracle worker, and I do not have the answers— they do. Dr. Albert Schweitzer said it well: "Each patient carries his own doctor inside him. They come to us not knowing that truth. We are at our best when we give the doctor who resides within each patient a chance to go to work."[4] The same is true in the healing of relationships.

Letting go of the desire to control, no longer looking to myself as the ultimate resource, I open up myself and others to the resources of God and the other parties. Together we open ourselves to be surprised by wisdom coming from the least expected sources. I know that the solution, which comes from the group, will be better than anything I have envisioned. Moreover, the parties will own it, feel good about it, be energized by it, and live out their commitment. I am responsible for the process, but even with the process I am always open to the suggestion of the parties as to what would be most helpful. In fact, I attempt to make each person feel as if they are responsible for the process as well.

Letting go of a desire to control is not being passive. It is trusting the Spirit, the wisdom of the group, and the process. It is being open to surprises and the possibility of miracles. It frees me up from the burden of feeling responsible for the outcome. It affirms that, like a child, I am part of the learning and growing circle.

In the midst of a facilitation, we also need to let go of our desire to control the conversation. As mediators we are present to serve the parties and their relationships. We are there to facilitate a good conversation. When that conversation is happening, the mediator can become a "potted plant," disappearing into the woodwork until needed again, letting the conversation flow. For example, two doctors were breaking up their practice, hardly talking with each other. The first and only question asked was: "What brought you together in the first place?" The doctors began to talk about how their relationship developed and about their first days of practice. They slowly began to laugh. All of a sudden they said to each other, "What are we fighting about? Let's continue to work together." They left arm in arm and never said thank you to the mediator. For a facilitator, it does not get any more successful than this, as you give up your desire for recognition and control.

Develop a Relationship of Respect and Trust

In Matthew 18 Jesus says, "Take care that you do not despise one of these little ones; for, I tell you, in heaven their angels continually see the face of my Father in heaven" (Matt. 18:10). Peterson paraphrases this to say that "their personal angels are constantly in touch with my Father in heaven." This is one of the most extraordinary scriptures in the Bible. How intimate and close to God! Children live in the presence of God as they are born knowing they are dependent and related. There is a natural sense of being interconnected and interdependent. Children know that it is all about relationships and "simple trust."

Seeking to be greater than another is driven by an autonomous, individualistic view of reality—a denial of the relational nature of life and the reality that we find our true selves in community. This view of reality is deeply ingrained in our culture. Being like a child is particularly countercultural for us. We live as if we believe that we are self-made.

Peacemakers, children of God, are those who know that it is all about relationships, with God, neighbor, and self. Our work is to help others notice this connectedness, as Carter Heyward suggests, and to reconstruct the relationship in ways that foster a mutual relation.[5] The most important work I do as a facilitator is to establish a genuine relationship with the parties. In preparation for the process, or in the beginning of the process, I spend as much time as needed with each party developing our relationship. This effort is motivated first of all by just plain curiosity about who the person is. Curiosity is based on the Latin word *cura*, meaning "care." The most important motivating factor for me is the respectful belief that each person is created in the image of God, has gifts and resources that can be discovered, and has qualities to which I can relate. In other words, the relationship must be based on genuine respect and caring for the other as a human being. I know that I must be authentic and real in my relationship with each of the parties. Often I find myself prayerfully opening space in myself for the other to enter into this relationship. Before I enter into the room with all the parties, I visualize each and pray for each. I can feel the Spirit creating connections as I provide space in myself for such relations.

In creating the relationship I know that I need to develop the trust of each party and do nothing in the process to destroy this trust. As trust develops, the parties begin to express their concerns and their needs. They begin to share their confidences. I never betray these confidences. In all I do, I am careful to be, in the words of Ron Kraybill, "impartial, fair, principled, and committed to the legitimate needs of all."[6] I am not an advocate for any party or any issue. As a facilitator, I am what Kraybill calls a "process advocate," advocating for "processes that uphold the dignity and equality of the people involved, involve all people affected by a decision in the decision-making process itself, give all participants equal access to information, ensure that participants are fully informed about their legal rights, and hold parties accountable for their commitments."[7]

In regard to relationships, I would add that we need to affirm ourselves, feeling comfortable in our skin, trusting our own instincts. Loving self is important to being able to love and care for another. This is sometimes the most difficult journey.

Bring a Sense of Gratitude and Abundance to the Process

A child has not earned anything. A child, who is a gift to the world, receives life as a gift, and the gift is sufficient and abundant. Each child is sacred, gifted, and great. The child sees life through eyes of wonder and awe. Hopefulness is natural and essential to a young child. Power and love are not limited by God. The child is not born with a sense of scarcity but may soon experience human-made scarcity. Seeking to be greater than another is driven by this fear of scarcity, a fear that there is never enough.

So how does that initial sense of abundance and giftedness express itself in the life of the peacebuilder? This affirmation of abundance begins with a vision of each person as a child of God, created in the image of God with gifts to be discovered and expressed in God's world. A peacebuilder provides a space, a time, and a process where people can feel empowered to find their own voice, tell their own stories, and find their own healing solution.

I begin each facilitation with an expression of gratitude to the parties for their courage and their wisdom in coming together and for their faith in their ability to resolve their differences. In the midst of all their fears and doubts, this affirmation begins to develop a sense of empowerment and hope. Throughout the mediation I recognize and affirm each moment of positive interaction and agreement.

The movement toward abundance is most clearly seen as we open up our imagination and creativity. We experience abundance when the parties brainstorm together and begin to see more options than they dreamed possible. In mediation theory, increasing the options is called "expanding the pie." Instead of seeing the pie through the eyes of scarcity, we begin to see that the pie is much bigger than we thought. There are not just two pieces that we were fighting over but many pieces available to us.

We see this abundance and creativity expressed in a playful spirit. Play is the activity of the child. Is not play, rather than work, the fullest expression of gratitude to God, gratitude for the gift of abundant life, which we have not earned or created ourselves, gratitude for the actions of God reconciling us and the cosmos to God's self? In our actions as co-creators with God of God's beloved community, are we not more like playful adventurers discovering, pointing to, and affirming by our actions God's gracious work in history? Does nonplayful work come out of a sense of what Parker Palmer calls "functional atheism," the belief that "nothing good is going to happen unless we make it happen"?[8] In playing, we are able to be creative and discover our true selves. For peacebuilders, this means that we need to bring a playful spirit, a lightness of being, to the process. This is important to opening up the imagination, the creative spirit in each person.

Play involves the whole being, including the body. Before entering into a facilitation, I always include physical exercise in my preparation, which is best considered play and not a burden. It is critical to releasing the tension in the body and being energized for the task. I also prayerfully open up in myself a space for the Spirit and for each person.

A sense of abundance enables a facilitator—a peacebuilder—to hold on to the hope that participants in a group can find a solution to the issues they face, or, at least, a better way of living together. When someone in a group I'm facilitating doesn't see a way out or wants to give up, I often tell the story about a friend named Dwight Harkin. Dr. Harkin, a heart surgeon, had a policy in the operating room: he would never give up until everyone in the room agreed that nothing else could be done. One day after hours of operating he finally agreed with his staff that he did not feel that he could save this patient's life. Consistent with his policy, he asked if anyone in the room felt he should try one more time. His staff said no. Then gradually an arm emerged from underneath the sheet. He tried one more time and saved the patient's life. My policy in a facilitation is the same. We don't give up until everyone agrees that there is nothing more we can do. This understanding is part of the relational covenant that I establish with the participants before we start. This understanding is helped by the parties knowing that we can take breaks, short breaks for a walk, or longer breaks for a night's sleep, before we continue on. It is not always easy to look and sound hopeful, but I find that it is important to energizing hope in the parties. The source of this hopefulness is a sense of abundance, not scarcity, in the relational life.

Another thing I always say to the parties in the beginning is to be patient, while I will be persistent. I let them know that there will be moments when they do not see any possible light at the end of the tunnel. In any conflict transformation process, the experience is like being on a roller coaster of emotions. With hopefulness and optimism, I continue to be persistent, gently and with care, until we reach a good place together or agree that we have done all we can. Even if we don't succeed, I check in with the parties periodically to see if they have new ideas or see new possibilities.

Express Humility as Awe and Wonder

The act of playing out of gratitude is, for me, the expression of humility experienced as wonder. This is being related to God, not believing we are gods. This comes from knowing that God is finally in control, not us, and that God's creation is worthy of awe and wonder. For me, this is what Jesus means when he asks us to become "humble like this child" (Matt. 18:4). This is not about humiliation or the acceptance of a subservient status. This is not about being inferior, or not feeling that you are great.

Recognizing that the God of wonder and awe is in control frees us from burdens that we do not need to carry—like the striving to be greater, trying to change anyone other than ourselves, and feeling that if I do not do it that it won't get done. Being humble is receiving life as a gift, not something that we have created.

Peacebuilders, children of God, live out of the sense of humility experienced as awe and wonder, wonder at the gifts of God in creation, the wisdom of the parties to resolve their own problems, and the ability of people to forge new relationships, to heal and reconcile. In all humility, peacebuilders can recognize their own limits, doubts, fears, sense of inadequacy, and even failures without feeling defeated or lacking in self-worth. Carolyn Schrock-Shenk, who is a teacher of peacebuilding and who was director of the Mennonite Conciliation Service, describes what this means for a peacebuilder: "It means recognizing my inadequacies, doubts and fears, and being honest about them. It means being ready to admit when I've 'blown' it and then picking myself up with grace and humility. It means being able to laugh at myself."[9]

Our sense of inadequacy leads us to rely more on God's power. Knowing about the log in our own eye, we do not bring a spirit of judgment to the people with whom we are working. We know that we only know in part and see things, like all human beings, in a mirror dimly (1 Cor. 13:12). We avoid the trap of thinking that our way, our process, is the only way. Humility creates authenticity.

In humility, peacebuilders see complexity as a friend—a friend to finding common ground and also a friend to truth. They avoid dualities and adopt more of a both/and approach to truth and relational life. They are open to criticism as being an opportunity for learning, evaluating what works and what does not. They are always flexible and open to suggestion. They avoid the problems of perfectionism. Peacebuilding is never about perfection. Perfectionists cannot accept the messiness, the ambiguity, and the limits of what can be achieved in peacebuilding. Psychologist Carl Rogers has said: "There is something I do before I start a session. I let myself know that I am enough. Not perfect. *Perfect wouldn't be enough.* But that I am human, and that is enough."[10]

Be in Solidarity with All Creation

The end result of being like a child is being in solidarity and community with God and neighbor, even the "enemy." We were made for community.

In Jesus' training manual for disciples, the Sermon on the Mount, he instructed his disciples, "Don't react violently against the one who is evil" (Matt. 5:39).[11] Instead; "Love your enemies and pray for those who persecute you" (Matt. 5:44). We are to be in community even with our enemies.

Does a sense of scarcity and striving for status and control destroy community by creating fear and anxiety? Doesn't this fear and anxiety lead to offenses and harm to others, particularly the "least"? Doesn't it create systems of domination and exploitation? Doesn't it create stumbling blocks, the literal meaning of the Greek word translated "sin"? Aren't there consequences? Jesus tells us: "If you give [children] a hard time, bullying or taking advantage of their simple trust, you'll soon wish you hadn't. You'd be better off dropped in the middle of the lake with a millstone around your neck. Doom to the world for giving these God-believing children a hard time! Hard times are inevitable, but you don't have to make it worse—and it's doomsday to you if you do" (Matt. 18:6-7, THE MESSAGE).

By juxtaposing the question of who is the greatest in heaven with the nature of being a child, Jesus opens up an examination of why we have destructive conflict and harm in this world. The source is our efforts to be greater than another, of trying to dominate or exploit others. Jesus tells us to recover the spirit of the child.

Peacemakers, children of God, are those who seek God's shalom: well-being and right relations for all creation. They see the humanity of the participants in any process and feel a connection with each person. They truly believe that human beings can come together and find connections with each other—common ground as well as higher ground. I do like Peterson's version of Matthew 5:9: "You're blessed when you can show people how to cooperate instead of compete or fight. That's when you discover who you really are, and your place in God's family" (THE MESSAGE). This is an extraordinary gift if we can help people who are in conflict discover who they really are and their place in God's family, with each other. We also, as peacebuilders, discover who we are and find wellness and wholeness in the process.

Summary of Virtues and Practices to Cultivate

To summarize, peacebuilders can and should cultivate these virtues and practices for the sake of the parties and for their own well-being.

Let Go of Striving for Status or Control

- Give up the desire to control the outcome.
- Let the conversation flow without feeling you need to control it.
- Give all the credit for any success to the participants.

Develop a Relationship of Respect and Trust with Each Party

- Help others see their interdependence and interconnection with each other.
- Spend as much time as needed with each party to develop a relationship of respect and trust, motivated by curiosity and genuine caring.
- Prayerfully open up space in one's self for the Spirit and each of the parties.
- Maintain confidences.
- Be impartial, fair, principled, and committed to the legitimate needs of all.
- Affirm yourself and trust your own instincts.

Bring a Sense of Gratitude and Abundance to the Process

- See each party as a child of God with unique gifts and resources.
- See yourself as a discoverer of the gifts and resources of the parties.
- Empower the parties to find their own voice, tell their own stories and find their own healing solution.
- Express gratitude to the parties for their courage and their wisdom in coming together and for their faith in being able to resolve their differences.
- Open up the imagination and abundant resources of the parties, helping them expand the pie.
- Bring a playful spirit, a lightness of being, to the process.
- Exercise before a process to relieve some of the tension in your own body.
- Be forever hopeful and optimistic that the parties can come to a better place together.
- Help the parties be patient, while you are persistent.

Express Humility as Wonder and Awe

- Recognize God is in control and the parties have the wisdom to resolve their own problems.

- Recognize your limits and even failures without feeling defeated or lacking in self-worth.
- Do not bring a spirit of judgment to the parties.
- Recognize the limits of one's vision.
- See complexity as a friend, avoiding dualities.
- Be open to suggestions and criticism.

Be in Solidarity with All Creation

- Seek well-being and right relations for all the parties.
- Believe the parties can find common ground and higher ground.
- Help create a new sense of relationship and community among the parties.

Be a Well: An Understanding of the Role of the Peacebuilder

Being well assists us in *being a well*, a resource to others. How we understand what it means to be a well is also critical to our ability to be well in the midst of conflict and truly be a resource to others. Our understanding of our role is critical to the success of our work. What are some of the role expectations and attitudes we want to avoid? What role expectations can lead to frustration and even to doing harm to those you are trying to help? Make a list of these.

I would include on this list Parker Palmer's "functional atheism," believing that ultimate responsibility rests with me. A "functional atheist" does not believe God is still active in history or that other people are working toward the same ends, but believes that if he or she does not do it, it will not get done.

We have already spoken about the need to abandon the need to control. Another way to talk about this is abandoning the need to be a miracle worker or a fixer. I don't know about you, but I have a hard enough time trying to fix my own problems. We all have felt the urge and believed we had the power to be the fixer. The motivation is a caring one, although it can carry with it a sense of superiority and the imposition of our will. The reality is that people can and must solve their own problems in order to own and be committed to the solution. We cannot bring about healing or reconciliation. We can only create the environment in which it can occur or the context for the Spirit to work. Trying to be a fixer is a burden that leads to frustration and even burnout.

Carolyn Schrock-Shenk speaks to my experience and to the heart of the issue of our understanding of our role and the consequences of our understanding:

> It is true . . . that this work can be draining. But it can also be very life-giving. Perhaps it is draining to the extent that I focus on "doing" rather than "being." In other words, perhaps the more I can abandon my need to control, to be the expert, and to fix others, the less drained I will be. The more that I can replace those with a quiet confidence that "in my weakness, God will be made strong," the more energized I will be.[12]

Triangulation is another difficulty. People come to us as peacebuilders, or as leaders, or just as fellow human beings and try to make their problem our problem. They want us to take their side. As discussed in chapter 2, we need to make sure people are doing all they can directly with the other party to reach a better place (Matt. 18:15) and to get involved with the two parties only when that fails, rather than being triangulated with any one party.

Let's try to understand what our role actually should be. Think about what has worked for you and was helpful to others. Make your own list.

My role as a peacebuilder has evolved into being a mediating presence, a person who is present between and among the parties, who brings people together in good conversation to solve their own problems and get to a better place together. The image of the well is helpful here. The well is the place around which people gather to meet and talk and fill their own vessels. As a peacebuilder, you can create the space or the environment in which the Spirit and the wisdom of the group can work.

What does it mean to be a mediating presence? These actions I associate with this role:

- Bring people together with their differences and their pain.
- Help create a sacred and safe space for conversation and dialogue, where the parties can bring their best selves to each other.
- Help develop a relational covenant as to how people want to be treated.
- Encourage the telling and hearing of stories.
- Encourage the use of the spiritual practices.

- Allow the parties to resolve their own conflicts, find healing, find justice and right relations, and reconcile with each other.

Ron Kraybill describes this role as the gift of accompaniment, "the art of being present to people in difficulty without rushing to fix things. . . . Accompaniment assumes that answers to serious trouble come in a process of reflection and learning, and that those who are in difficulty must find the answers themselves."[13]

This role will be fleshed out in the next six chapters as we explore how we engage others in conflict transformation/peacebuilding. I hope that as you experience this role description, you feel your body relaxing, a burden being removed from your shoulders, and a sense of excitement about playing the role of the mediating presence, not the fixer.

We can all play this role even when we are a party to the conflict. We might not be able to be the mediator or facilitator, but we can bring this spirit to our involvement in the process.

In JustPeace, we have developed this rubric in our work:

TRUST GOD
TRUST YOURSELF
TRUST THE WISDOM OF OTHERS
TRUST THE PROCESS

Conclusion

We can and need to prepare ourselves for being constructive in engaging others in conflict transformation/peacebuilding. We will never be fully prepared. This journey of preparation is a journey we will continue to be on for our lifetime. It is not about perfection. It is about being human. We will learn from each engagement. We will continue to grow. All this preparation is not an end in itself, but in this relational world we are preparing ourselves to be engaged with others in a way that heals relationships and creates a new sense of community.

PART TWO

Engaging Others in Conflict Transformation

FIVE

Designing Good Process
The Circle Process

Create a common well together.

∽◉〜

*Design a circle process for a good conversation to get
to a better place together.*

How do we engage people with whom we are in conflict? How do
we facilitate the engagement of others who are in conflict? In this
chapter we examine the theory and design of good process, a process that
provides space where we can have a good conversation to get to a better
place together.

Digging a well, at least for most of human time on this earth, was
a collaborative venture. For many communities in the world, it still is.
For these communities, the well is not only a place to receive life-giving
water but also a place of meeting, a place of conversation. The circle and
the circle process have become for me such a well, a place where we can
bring our fears, our wounds, our deepest values, and where we can experience learning, healing, solutions to our issues, and a new relationship
with one another.

The Goal: Good Conversation to Get to a Better Place Together

In her book *Turning to One Another: Simple Conversations to Restore Hope to the Future*, Margaret Wheatley talks about how we can change the world through "simple, truthful conversation where we each have a chance to speak, we each feel heard, and we each listen well." She goes on to say, "This is how great changes begin, when people begin talking to each other about their experiences, hopes, and fears."[1]

Two women sit down together in Vermont at a kitchen table. They begin to talk about land mines. They discover that each feels passionately about the subject and wants to do something to remove these land mines from the earth, where they continue to maim and kill innocent people. They start an organization, which becomes international. They receive the Nobel Peace Prize. This journey began with a simple, human conversation at the kitchen table. Mothers who have lost children to drunk drivers start talking. They want to do something to curb drunk driving. Out of these conversations grows an organization, Mothers Against Drunk Driving. They make a difference.

We could share many stories of such conversations that lead to constructive change in this world. In fact, all such change begins with some conversation. Meg Wheatley wants us all to be involved in such conversations: "I wrote this book to encourage and support you to begin conversations about things that are important to you."[2] She feels such conversations are the only way out of our growing isolation from each other and the only way to change our world for the better.

Such conversations are the goal of all our engagements. I am simply talking about good conversations that move those in conflict to a better place together. Remembering this as our goal helps us design processes conducive to such a conversation and reminds us to get out of the way when such a conversation begins to flow.

This chapter is about how to start such a conversation when the parties have not been able to talk directly with each other, where barriers to such a conversation exist. Having these conversations around the kitchen table is hard enough, but having these conversations in the midst of conflict is daunting for most where trust is low, and anxiety and fear are high. We are talking about how to create a process that allows each person to tell their story. We are also reflecting on how to move such conversations from the kitchen table to church meetings, to boardrooms—to larger conversations where facilitation is needed. In short, we are talking here about a facilitated conversation.

In JustPeace, we use the term *facilitated conversation* to describe what we are doing. We use this term instead of *mediation,* as much of our work in the church involves values and deals with harm. People do not like to enter into a process thinking they are mediating their values, but they can and will talk about them. People also do not want to mediate their harm, but they will talk about their harm, where there is a process for addressing their harm. Describing an engagement as a facilitated conversation is broad enough to describe mediation, or negotiation, or dialogue, or a consensus-building process or simply a healing conversation. Such facilitated conversations draw on lessons learned from the theory and practice of all these fields, but we always describe what we are doing as a facilitated conversation, regardless of the issue or the process.

Process: The Theory of Collaborative Process

In a relational world, the process we use to deal with a conflict is as important as, or more important than, any solution. "You can't get to a good place in a bad way."[3] The way decisions are made is critical to the ownership and success of the decision. Generally people can live with a decision they may not actually prefer if they have had a voice in that decision or resolution. Everyone needs to feel valued, and to be treated fairly.

Bad process can be a source of conflict, yielding resentment, feelings of being treated unfairly, and a sense of powerlessness. When we are asked to intervene in a conflict, we need to find out if part of the present conflict is a result of bad process in the past. We do not want to compound any conflict by developing a process that leaves people feeling worse than they did before.

Collaborative Process: The Theory

A collaborative approach to a facilitated conversation is different from an adversarial approach, the process of the courtroom. The chart on the next page expresses some of the differences.

I like to tell parties in a facilitated conversation that the matter is in their hands. They get to make the decision. Nothing happens unless they agree. I have not found anyone who does not prefer to retain control over their future rather than turning it over to a third party through an adversarial process.

Comparison of Adversarial Process	vs.	Collaborative Process
Third party makes decisions		Parties make decisions
Looks to the past		Looks to future
Focuses on facts		Focuses on relationships
Seeks to establish liability/fault		Seeks to restructure relationship
Results in winner and loser		Results in accommodative resolution – win/win

The past is important, but the present and future are even more important. Adversarial process can focus only on the past. For example, did you do it, and how should you be punished? Collaborative process takes the past seriously, but it incorporates the past in a new future.

Collaboration focuses primarily on the relationship: facts are seen in the context of the relationship and the future; the parties seek to restructure the relationship, including personal accountability, not just imposed liability or fault. Finally, collaboration works to meet everyone's needs and interests, instead of to declare one person the winner and the other the loser. The adversarial system is still necessary as a very sophisticated backup system when parties are unsuccessful at collaborating. The best and first approach, however, should be a collaborative process.

The chart at the top of the next page outlines the basic theory supporting collaborative process. A collaborative process, as depicted in this chart, involves a high degree of commitment to both personal goals (empowerment of self) and relationships (recognition of the other). We can serve both personal and relational goals. "Avoiding" the conflict does not take seriously either our commitment to ourselves or each other. "Accommodating" takes the relationship seriously but not oneself. We need to expose and rid ourselves of "doormat" theology, where people sacrifice themselves and their needs for the relationship. "Competitive" focuses on winning for the self but does nothing for the relationship.

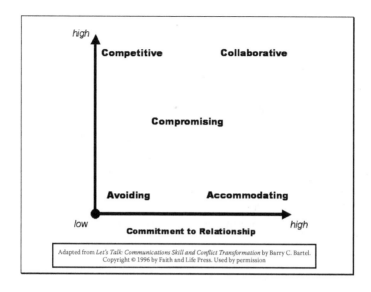

"Compromising" is a step in the right direction, but "collaboration" is where the needs and interests of the self and the other (the relationship) are both addressed and attempts are made to satisfy each (win/win).

Bush and Folger, in *The Promise of Mediation,* assert that mediation should work toward two goals: empowerment of each party and recognition by each party of the other.[4] You can see how these two movements come together in the chart above where both personal goals and relationships are affirmed. Conflict often unsettles equilibrium, causing people to feel powerless. Bush and Folger point out that through the interplay of both movements, people regain balance in conflict. Empowerment comes from knowing/feeling one has been heard. It frees parties to be able to recognize (affirm, appreciate) the other even though they may disagree. It even frees people to "change their minds." Contrast for yourself the emotions that emerge when you feel empowered and when you feel disempowered, and when you are affirmed and when you are not affirmed.

The principal work in a collaborative approach is to empower the parties, enabling them to feel calmer, clearer, more confident, more organized. With a greater sense of equilibrium, they can be resourceful and open to recognizing the other. Empowerment allows people to move away from a self-protective, self-absorbed, defensive, suspicious posture, unable to look beyond their own needs. Empowerment allows individuals to become more open, reflective, attentive, and responsive. These capacities make appreciation and affirmation of the other possible.

And this kind of shift is a significant achievement, whether or not a solution results. Usually, however, solutions flow when the parties experience mutual empowerment and recognition.

Circle Process: A Way

When I began to move from the two adversarial tables of the courtroom to the one table of collaborative conversation, I searched for a process that would be most consistent with the theology and practices of the faith. What does a faith-based conflict transformation process look like? Consistent with the reflections in the first four chapters, I was trying to understand how to create the space and the time where people can

- find sacred space, a relatively safe space;
- recognize their interdependence and connection;
- find a sense of equality and respect;
- have voice—even the quiet ones;
- experience deep listening and respectful speaking;
- feel responsible and accountable for the outcome;
- solve their problems and find healing.

The answer came from many sources, all about the same time. I heard about circles from Chief Justice Yazzi of the Navaho Nation. He and I were both board members of the *Journal of Law and Religion.* As chief justice, he followed the laws and practices of the American judicial system. However, he realized that the adversarial retributive system was not healing the people of his nation, especially the youth. He then returned to the ancient process of his own people, Peacebuilding Circles, and gave people the opportunity to choose which process they wanted.

I also heard about circles from my study of restorative justice with Howard Zehr at Eastern Mennonite University. There I was introduced to the work of Judge Barry Stuart, who started using First Nation circle processes in his courtroom in the Yukon. In a meeting with one of the general secretaries of our church, he reported that he had just had the most powerful conversation he had ever experienced, using something called "the circle process" that Meg Wheatley was using with all her work. Finally, I came to know Kay Pranis, who was the restorative justice planner for the Minnesota Department of Corrections. She became my teacher, and her books *Peacemaking Circles: From Crime to Community* with Barry Stuart and Mark Wedge, and *The Little Book of Circle Processes: A New/*

Old Approach to Peacemaking were transformative for me.[5] Kay taught me that circles combine the ancient traditions, for example, of Native Americans, "with contemporary concepts of democracy and inclusivity in a complex, multicultural society."[6]

In short, I found the circle process a great gift to the church and the world. As one participant said, "The circle process has helped bring us back to a better and more faithful way of being church."

The Theology of the Circle

Sitting in circle expresses in a physical and symbolic way the interconnectedness, interdependence, and unity of all life as found in God, with deep appreciation for diversity and the unique wisdom and contribution of each person. Everyone in the circle is the alpha and omega of the circle, with equal responsibility and accountability for the work of the circle.

The circle emphasizes collective and communal wisdom and discernment. We are all on the same side of the table. The circle becomes a place to practice the Great Commandment, which is the sum of the law and the prophets: loving God, neighbor, and self. It is all about relationships, the healing of relationships and the formation of community. The circle symbolizes and establishes the community we want to be. My understanding is the circle is the strongest shape in creation, stronger than anything that has corners. The circle can become a spiral as the circle moves deeper and deeper.

The Ritual of the Circle

One of the more obvious connections of circle process and the rhythms of church life is that in circle process, opening and closing rituals frame the whole time and space together as sacred. The circle is a sacred space. In fact, circle process calls the church back from doing business like the Chamber of Commerce, to doing "worshipful work," and seeing its task to discern in and through community the will of God. Circle process has helped me understand again the power of ritual to transform lives and create community. At the center of the circle is a continuous reminder(s) of the presence of God, for example a candle. Ritual helps create a space safe enough, physically and emotionally, for the telling of our stories and the speaking and hearing of truth.

Guidelines or Relational Covenants for the Circle

Circle process involves the participants in defining how individuals should be treated in the conversation and life of the circle. These guidelines are best expressed, in the theology and tradition of the church, by the word "covenant," a mutual agreement that binds people together, honors the other party, and requires mutual accountability and responsibility. I have found the creating and living out of such covenants the most important act that can be taken to prevent destructive conflict. There is no better definition of such relational covenants than the one Kay Pranis taught me: "Shared values in action, expressed in a practical manner."

The Talking Piece

The use of a talking piece in the circle is the most helpful ritual I know to encourage deep listening and respectful speaking. The talking piece enables everyone to have a voice, including the quiet ones, often the wisest, and enables the talkers to listen. When you hold the talking piece, you get to talk and everyone else gets to listen. The talking piece goes from left to right around the circle, giving everyone the opportunity to speak without interruption. A person can pass for any reason, including feeling too emotional to talk or feeling what they wanted to say has already been said. The talking piece is something respected by the community. In Native American circles, a feather is often the talking piece. The Bible is the talking piece I most often use, but only when the group finds it appropriate. The talking piece is used wisely and not mechanically, with the facilitator moving as needed between passing it and holding it with open conversation, one at a time, in the circle. The talking piece removes much of the burden of facilitation from the facilitator. The steward on occasion will speak without the talking piece, but only rarely in my experience. For me, the circle process is easier to practice than other forms of facilitation, in large part because of the use of the talking piece.

Consensus Decision Making

Circle process is grounded in the value of consensus and provides an alternative to the church's use of parliamentary procedure, with its debate and adversarial format of winners and losers. My experience of trying to deal with controversial issues by majority vote is that the issue is not fully resolved. The minority, the losers, keep working to subvert the majority decision. The Quakers see such voting as a form of violence against the humanity and integrity of the minority, not valuing "that of God in every person." Coming to consensus for Quakers is a way of communal discernment of the will of God.

Circles and consensus decision making have given the church a way to practice holy conferencing and spiritual discernment. A consensus process encourages greater participation in making and carrying out decisions. Broadly based participation draws out the rich variety of ideas and resources necessary to deal with difficult problems in a holistic manner. I understand consensus as a process of seeking the common mind without resort to a formal vote, engaging in genuine dialogue that is respectful, mutually supportive, and empowering while seeking to discern God's will. Consensus, which is not the same as unanimity, is declared when one of the following occurs: all are in agreement about an outcome; or most are in agreement and the few for whom it is not their first preference, nonetheless accept they have been fairly heard and can live with that outcome. Another way to put this is to say that a consensus is reached when no one feels a need to oppose it. This process involves everyone seeking alternatives that address everyone's concerns and interests, something greater (higher ground) than anyone's preconceived ideas (newness). Once a consensus is reached, there is communal ownership, and more effective and sustainable agreements.

Leadership—the Steward of the Circle

The concept of the "guardian" or "keeper of the circle," terms used in Native American circles, liberates leaders or facilitators from the burden of thinking they alone must fix or solve the problems being dealt with in the circle, or heal the relationships that are broken. Critical to the concept is the recognition that everyone in the circle is responsible for the good work of the circle. The concept is congruent with an understanding of servant leadership. Instead of "guardian" or "keeper" of the circle, I have used the term "steward" for such servant leadership, a term that is more familiar in the church. Stewardship involves caring for what is entrusted to you. A circle steward is one who helps create and monitor the sacred space and time for dialogue where the community can solve its own problems and experience together healing. The steward does this work by:

- setting a tone of respect and hope that honors and supports every participant;
- framing the circle as sacred by beginning and ending with ritual;

- obtaining agreement on the relational covenant;
- raising powerful questions and issues to address before passing the talking piece;
- encouraging the telling and hearing of stories;
- helping everyone practice listening for understanding, speaking the truth in love, using their imagination to reach higher ground, and being forgiving;
- at the end of passing the talking piece, or at other times as needed, summarizing the contributions of the circle;
- allowing participants in the circle to resolve their own conflicts, find healing, justice, and right relations, and even reconcile with one another.

Often there are two stewards, not just one. Two heads are often better than one. Different styles and experiences come together to provide greater knowledge, skills, and insights. A balance in terms of diversity can assist parties in feeling more comfortable, especially in conflicts involving race, ethnicity, or gender. Co-stewards can take turns and divide up the work. One may focus more on issues and facts while the other focuses on feelings or emotions, or one can lead and direct the process while the other monitors and ensures that important elements are not overlooked.

The Use of Circles

Circles, as described above, have the capacity, for example, to transform the way we make decisions, the way we conduct our grievance procedures, even the way we experience Holy Communion as the ritual of reconciliation and the healing of relationships.

I invited Judge Barry Stuart and Kay Pranis to a conference on restorative justice at the federal courthouse in Boston. A group of youth from Chelsea and Revere in Massachusetts came to the conference. They were part of a program called Roca, "a youth development organization committed to serving the most disenfranchised and disengaged young people ages 14–24 (street/court/gang involved; drop-outs; young parents; and refugees and immigrants)."[7] These young people developed a mutual admiration society with Barry and Kay. They wanted to be trained in circles. Barry and Kay worked with them, along with tribal elders from the Yukon. As a result, these young people have trained hundreds of other young people in circle process, and conducted circles with each other, their parents, the police chief, the superintendent of schools, just to name a few.

One of the most moving stories that has come out of Roca involved the death of Desi Kimmon, a twelve-year-old killed in a hit-and-run auto accident. Everyone was devastated. The staff, in the words of the director, did not know what to do. Being exhausted and emotionally drained, the staff just hoped that not too many young people would show up at Desi's wake. They did show up, all of them, and a group of young women, age thirteen, demanded they all go back to Roca and have a circle so they could talk about Desi and grieve together. Angie Rodriguez, the staff member present, said, "They ran the circle. They put Desi's picture on the floor. . . . One of the girls put a special thing that was hers because her mother passed away and they used that as the talking piece. . . . They did guidelines on a flip chart with markers, different colors. They burned sage, they took Desi's picture and put the sage around it and smudged it. Then they started with an opening and a closing . . . I didn't have to do anything . . . they just did it." [8]

Several years ago, on the first day of a Peace Camp, I talked with the young people about circles. I then left the next day. I later learned that on the fourth day of the camp, displeased with the way the camp was being run, the young people said that they wanted a circle with the director and the staff so they could explain their concerns. They turned to an African-American district superintendent and said, "We trust you. We want you to be our steward." That night they all sat on the floor in circle. They not only planned the program for the rest of the camp, but they also planned the camp for the next year.

The point here is not just that young people get it but that circles are not only for conflicts. The circle is a vessel for grieving together, for healing, for talking through an issue, for making decisions, for working through difficult conversations, for dealing with conflicted situations, for developing a team, and for celebrating together. I have used circles of eight to ten people in a gathering of a thousand people, where each circle determined their best ideas to share with the whole group, which then worked as a whole to consensus. My brother often uses the process when a family comes to his office for counseling. For Roca, it has become a way of life.

Preparation for the Circle

Preparation for the circle—the work done before the circle comes together—is critical to success, especially for a circle dealing with conflict.

The Importance of Early Engagement

If conflict is not engaged early, there is greater potential for escalation of tensions in which the person is seen as the problem; issues multiply and become generalized; other people are dragged into the conflict (triangulation); people become reactive (eye for an eye); and opposition grows to the extremes. Early engagement of conflict in a constructive way can de-escalate tension, decrease the chances for violence, maintain the ability to trust, ensure better communication as difficult issues are discussed, and prevent person-to-person contact from becoming less direct.

The Preparation

Preparation is key. Preparation is critical to understanding the issues, the people involved, and the structures within which the conflict developed. The preparation time is also the time when you create credibility and trust with all the parties. Finally, it is the time when the circle is designed, so that agreement is reached on the primary focus of the circle, who will be present, what will be included in the relational covenant, and when and where the circle will meet. The following overview will be fleshed out in subsequent chapters.

Analysis

Begin by talking with the key players. These discussions create a relationship of trust and bringing people to the table. Learn as much as you can about the issues, problems, concerns, and interests underlying the problems as well as the hopes for what might be accomplished together. Ask for ideas about how to make the process constructive. Make sure all sides feel heard. In large interventions in a church, for example, a survey instrument can be useful for gathering input and giving voice to many people. Sometimes I bring like-minded people together in affinity circles to talk in response to the types of questions described above. These circles allow people to vent, focus on the underlying issues and concerns, and develop together their hopes for a constructive outcome. Affinity circles also educate participants in the circle process. Participants in these circles can assist in choosing who should be in the joint circle.

Selecting Participants for the Circle

Ask the key players who they would like to see in the circle. A circle works best with eight to twelve people, but I have facilitated much larger circles. Here is an example: in a facilitation of a complaint against a pastor for stealing money, the circle might include members of the church who have been harmed; the district superintendent and a member of the board of ordained ministry, who represent the covenant of ministry that has been breached; the minister and the minister's spouse; their best friends; and an ex-offender.

In a dispute between two churches, we had five representatives of each church in the circle surrounded by another four hundred people, who understood that their only role was to listen. In this circle, we provided complete transparency.

Ideally each circle includes those affected by the conflict, those who might block any decision if they were not in the circle, as well as those who can bring wisdom to the process. Make sure that everyone knows who will be in the circle so there are no surprises.

Understanding of the Process and the Role of the Facilitator

The persons who are going to be part of the circle need to understand the circle process and the role of the facilitator or steward of the circle. Discuss the use of ritual, the talking piece, and the consensus nature of the decision-making process. Ask the participants what they would like to use as a talking piece. Together work out a relational covenant as to how they all want to be treated in the process, which includes confidentiality when that is required. Agree on a date and a place for meeting. Come to an understanding of the focus of the circle.

Conclusion

Every once in a while I look back on my life in the courtroom and I wonder how this trial lawyer came to appreciate the work of circles. Nothing could have been further from my experience and training. For many of you, sitting in circle is something you have done all your life, around the living room and at church meetings. You might wonder what is added by the use of ritual, covenant, and the talking piece, for example. For others, sitting in circle facing each other and talking about the deep issues in your life might seem totally foreign and the last thing you want to do. All I ask you to do is try it.

I tried the circle process with our church covenant group at our first meeting following summer vacation. At that session we were simply catching up with one another. Several people commented, "I wish that we had tried this at our family reunion." In the midst of conflict, the circle process becomes an expanding vessel with the capacity to incorporate new learnings.

The next five chapters will open up in greater depth each aspect of the circle process and will show how each element is important to the design of good process, whether or not the work is done in circle.

SIX

Creating Ritual and Covenants

Share the well.

*Together open yourselves to God through ritual and to
each other through a relational covenant.*

The use of ritual and a relational covenant can make the circle a
space safe enough—physically and emotionally—for speaking and
hearing truth. The well of the circle is sacred and can provide healing
waters as we share the well together.

What is a ritual, and why is it so important in our lives? How do we
develop rituals in the midst of conflict that open everyone to the presence of God and to the best they can be?

Importance of Rituals

Our lives are filled with rituals from simple family rituals around meals
and Thanksgiving to deep rituals, for example, of baptisms, weddings,
funerals, and daily and weekly worship.

Tom Driver says that rituals at their best provide for order, community, and transformation.[1] In a world that seems chaotic, rituals give order to our lives, an order that is freeing and not life denying, that helps us speak our truth, be authentic, find focus and direction. In a world where we often feel isolated and alienated, rituals bring us together and help us create community. In a world where we seem stuck, rituals help us open ourselves to growth, to learning, to transformation. The circle embodies this. The relational covenant and the talking piece are ritual elements in creating order. The circle and its rituals embody community with God and neighbor. The journey is one of transformation—bringing into being what we need and hope for—right relationship.

Marcia McFee, a teacher and leader in designing liturgies and rituals, explains how ritual allows us to deal with our liminality.[2] The word *liminality* comes from the Latin word for "threshold." Liminality is the experience of being on the threshold between the past and future, feeling and being betwixt and between. We see this most clearly in our rites of passage, such as baptism, marriage, and funeral services. The ritual of baptism moves an individual from being the child of parents to recognizing that she or he is a child of God. The ritual of marriage moves individuals from being single to being in a covenant relationship for life. The funeral service recognizes the movement of the deceased from life through death to life in the spirit with God, as well as acknowledges the movement beginning in those who grieve from a sense of deep loss to hope in the resurrection.

Liminality is clearly experienced in conflict. As McFee describes, we stand between an old relationship and identity that no longer exists and a newly defined relationship or identity which is not yet. We have lost a sense of order and also a sense of community. We feel uncertain and uneasy. We feel disempowered and not recognized. How do we get through the threshold of this experience to a new order, a new relationship, a new identity?

The circle process is a rite of passage, a sacred journey, where we strive for this new order, this new relationship, this new identity. Rituals are not magic. We are not passing a magic wand over the conflict. We should also recognize that rituals can be constructive or destructive. There are rituals created for the courtroom and rituals created for the circle. What is the difference? How do we create rituals that fill us with the Spirit, give us meaning, and bring us together?

The Ritual of the Courtroom

Rituals were a significant part of my life as a lawyer. When I entered the courtroom as a trial lawyer, I passed a bar, a railing that separated the players in the courtroom's drama from the spectators and the witnesses in the case. I went to one of two tables, and the opposing attorney sat at the other table. Everyone was told to rise when the judge, dressed in a robe, entered the courtroom. The judge sat behind an elevated bench, the highest structure in the courtroom. We all proceeded according to a variety of rituals about when and how to speak, how to approach the judge, how to address the jury. These rituals provide a backdrop for understanding the rituals of the circle process.

Rituals of the Circle

The Circle as Ritual Symbol

In circle we are sitting together, not at separate tables. In mediation, for example, we attempt through the process to move the parties emotionally from different sides of the table to the same side, looking at the same issues, the same interests and needs, with the task of trying to meet the interests and needs of all the parties. In circle, we start on the same side of the table, as there are no sides. Everyone is facing each other and equidistant from the center. By being in circle we all become the alpha and omega of the circle, recognizing that we are all interconnected and interdependent. Everyone has equal voice. Everyone is also equally responsible for the outcome of the work of the circle. The circle is about collective wisdom and discernment. In short, we embody by being in the circle the community we want to create.

Rituals shape us and form us. Michael Glennon, a victim witness advocate at Roca, comments: "The more you are in circle, physically sitting in circle, the more you get to be in circle when you're not in circle."[3] Another way to put this is to say that the circle is not a onetime experience. In conflict transformation, we are hoping to do more than solve a particular problem or heal a particular conflict. One of the goals of the circle is to create a new way of living, a new way of relating to each other, a new way of engaging conflicts in the future.

A Ritual Table

A small round table in the middle of the circle provides a centering focus for the group, with ritual symbols and ritual objects on the table. The table should be small so that it does not obstruct the view of anyone in the circle of the other participants and does not create a barrier in the emotional and physical space of the circle.

I am speaking from my own experience, with the understanding that different cultures will have different symbols and objects and that the creativity of each group will choose what is right for that group. In fact, I always ask the parties to make suggestions as to what would be most helpful to them in remembering who they are and whose they are. I have found that all the groups I have worked with like to have a candle in the center, reminding them of the presence of the Spirit and the illumination they hope to receive as a group. As I have grown to understand more fully the reconciling, restoring power of bread and wine in Holy Communion, I have found groups wanting to have the cup and the bread at the center of their work. We will develop this more fully in the last chapter.

Two churches were at war with each other. One church had been in existence for over one hundred years. Behind this church was a large cemetery. The church had membership of a few hundred. This old country church found the city spreading out and around it. Another United Methodist church bought land a mile away. This church already had several thousand members and was growing. The old country church was deeply threatened.

A war developed between these two congregations to the point where they were sending e-mail viruses to each other. I spent time with each congregation, listening to their concerns and hopes. We then gathered a circle of five representatives from each church, surrounded by the members of both churches, about four hundred people whose only job was to listen. We decided that all ten people would bring something to share in the circle that symbolized why they loved their church. There were, for example, posters for programs, worship bulletins, annual reports.

One member of the "country church" brought an electrical plug. I was eager to hear why! When it was his turn to describe what he had brought and its importance to him, he explained, "When I joined this church, I was asked to help one of the senior members of the church rewire the church. From him, I learned all I know about electrical wiring, but, more importantly, I learned what it meant to be church." This plug and all the other objects on the table in the center of the circle became a ritual affirmation of each church and reminded everyone throughout the evening what was best about these churches that they were trying to affirm together.

The Talking Piece

The talking piece is a ritual device that assists the spiritual practices of (1) listening for understanding and (2) speaking the truth in love. The practice is simple. When you hold the talking piece, you speak without interruption. When you don't hold the talking piece, you listen. You can pass for any reason, including having nothing to add or being too emotional to speak at that particular moment.

In my practice, which I learned from a Native American tradition, the talking piece passes to my left clockwise around the circle, as the earth goes around the sun. With this order, people know when they are going to talk. Without this order, people often continue to sit on the edge of their chairs waiting to respond in kind to anything with which they disagree, especially negative statements about themselves. My experience is that in waiting on the talking piece you find that others respond, for example, to an attack on you in ways better than anything you could say and in ways that are better heard by the person who attacked you.

There are other methods, like the invitational method of Eric Law, an Episcopal priest, in which the speaker passes the talking piece to anyone in the group that he or she chooses.[4] I like going in order, especially in the beginning of the circle, so everyone knows when they will speak and can relax and listen until that time comes when they hold the talking piece. I find the invitational method works best later in the circle after everyone has had their say and when a member of the circle wants to hear from a specific person.

There should be nothing mechanical about any of the rituals of the circle, including the talking piece. We should remember that the purpose of all we are doing, in the midst of conflict, is to help people have a good conversation to get to a better place. Once the deep emotions have been expressed and people have told their stories, the conversation does begin to flow. When I see that the conversation is developing, I often put the talking piece in the center of the circle. I say, "Let's just talk together with the understanding that no one interrupts another person when he or she is talking." If the conversation gets stuck, emotions are blocking a conversation, or voices are not being heard, I pick up the talking piece, ask a question, and pass the talking piece to the left around the circle.

I have not found any ritual or technique more powerful than the use of a talking piece in encouraging people to listen well and also to speak well. Knowing you are going to speak without interruption and in sequence around the circle reduces your anxiety and improves your ability to listen. It slows down the pace of the conversation so that people can be more reflective and thoughtful. The talking piece also insures that we will hear from everyone, including the quiet ones whose wisdom is not always heard. The talking piece does create order and community. Often I hear people say that they experience transformation in their emotions and their thoughts as they hold the talking piece.

What talking piece should be used? The talking piece should be something of significance to the group and that the group respects. In some Native American circles, a feather is used. The talking piece that groups have used most often in my practice is the Bible. There is a very different feel about the use of the Bible in the circle and the use of the Bible in court as a witness swears to tell the truth. However, I have found groups that did not want to use the Bible. I was leading a circle in a seminary. I asked the group if it was acceptable to them to use the Bible. Two women in the circle said the Bible had been used to oppress them, and they did not feel comfortable using it. They suggested, instead, that we use a flower out of a bouquet of flowers found in the room. Everyone found this acceptable. Circles have chosen, for example, a shell, a rock, a wooden cross, a candle, a piece of salt, a set of keys. I always get the approval of the group before any specific talking piece is used.

The Steward of the Circle as Ritual Leader

The steward is the ritual leader of the circle. As religious people, we are involved in one way or another in leading and participating in worship services. As steward, recognizing that in a circle everyone shares leadership, you can ask others to help you plan and lead the opening and closing rituals, rituals that frame the whole time and space together as sacred. These rituals must be carefully conceived so they are not manipulative or coercive. No one should feel the ritual is a judgment on their behavior or that it takes the other's side. Finally it needs to be brief, not a sermon, not a worship service. The parties are ready to talk. They have much to say. Do not get them frustrated with long rituals.

Opening Ritual

The opening ritual involves the recognition that we are not alone, God is with us. Here we open ourselves to God, God's guidance and the creativity of the Spirit. In doing so, we name and frame the space where we come together to transform our conflicts as sacred space. In the opening ritual we recognize we are shifting the focus from our separateness to our interconnection and interdependence. We are defining the space as a place where we can tell our stories and be authentic. We also recognize that here we have the possibility of finding higher ground, not just common ground.

I usually begin by reading scripture, for example, Jeremiah 18:1-4 about the potter reworking a vessel: we humans can create another "vessel," another relationship, that seems good to God. Then I pray, such as, "Gracious God, who heals all wounds, give us ears to hear and understand each other, eyes to see each other as you see us, and a heart that is open to being transformed by your Spirit. Amen."

Stephanie Hixon, with whom I work, often starts by singing a song that calms and centers everyone. Then she prays. If I sang, the conflict would then be with me! Everyone's skills and talents are different. Use the talents, skills, and creativity you have in the ritual life of the circle.

Closing Ritual

This is a time to affirm what has been accomplished in the group. Regardless of what happens in the circle, the closing is an opportunity to express appreciation for the contributions of everyone. The closing ritual is a time to ask for continuing guidance and support and to name the fact that the participants are moving out of the circle, back into the ordinary space of their daily lives.

Relational Covenant

During the first week of the existence of JustPeace, I received a call from a layperson in a church in Minnesota. He described the troubled life of his church. Nothing ever happened at meetings. Everything happened in parking lots, over the telephone lines and the Internet. The church was deeply divided and conflicted. As a church, the members decided to study Matthew 18 together. They then created a relational covenant based on Matthew 18: a guideline for how members of the church should treat each other. After this good work, he said the church was peaceful and had no conflicts. Now I am sure they had conflicts, but what he was saying was these conflicts were being dealt with constructively within the relational covenant that they had established. A relational covenant made a difference.

I have become convinced that developing a relational covenant is one of the most important things we can do to prevent destructive conflict. I believe this is true for circles as well as for all our committees and church institutions. Such covenants are critical to creating and nurturing community. If being the body of Christ is the primary goal of the church, then creating and living out these covenants is as important, if not more important, than any other decisions that are made. Conflicts are still present, but they are engaged constructively.

Below we will explore the use of relational covenants in circles. We also will reflect on their use in all institutions, helping to shape the culture of an institution to be more like the beloved community we desire.

Biblical Covenants

In studying mediation, I was taught about guidelines, such as not interrupting each other. The guidelines generally defined negative conduct to be avoided. As I began to conduct facilitated conversations in faith-based communities and to think about how our biblical theology informs this work, I reflected on the biblical concept of covenant. How might the biblical understanding of covenant give greater depth to the movement to create guidelines to regulate or transform our behavior?

In the Bible, "covenant" defines relationships between God and humankind and also between neighbors. The biblical experiences of God were always in covenant relationships, beginning with God's covenant with Noah: "I establish my covenant with you, that never again shall all flesh be cut off by the waters of a flood, and never again shall there be a flood to destroy the earth" (Gen. 9:11). God established a covenant with Abraham: "I will make of you a great nation, and I will bless you, and make your name great, so that you will be a blessing" (Gen. 12:2). The most important covenant in the Hebrew Bible is with Israel. "Know therefore that the LORD your God is God, the faithful God who maintains covenant loyalty with those who love him and keep his commandments" (Deut. 7:9). For Christians, the covenant with Jesus Christ built on and fulfilled the covenants with God that preceded it. "Then he took a cup, and after giving thanks he gave it to them, saying, 'Drink from it, all of you; for this is my blood of the covenant, which is poured out for many for the forgiveness of sins'" (Matt. 26:27-28).

In the Bible there are also covenants between people. These covenant were, in the words of Jonathan Sacks, a response to the question: "How can we establish relationships secure enough to become the basis of co-operation, without the use of economic, political or military power? . . . Covenant is the attempt to create partnership without dominance or submission."[5] The covenant is based on honoring the other. At the heart of the covenant is an understanding of mutual accountability and responsibility. At the heart of covenantal theology is an understanding of a God who keeps covenant promises even when other parties to the covenant—human beings—do not. God's never-ceasing love keeps restoring us to a covenant relationship.

Relational covenants emphasize the relational nature of our understanding of how we should be treated in community, and recognize that this relationship with each other is embedded in the covenant God has made with God's creation. The covenant expresses our greatest values and give us a structure in which we can address relational brokenness. As people called to imitate God, the covenant is one that we continually and lovingly work to restore when it is broken. This understanding significantly affects how we react to breaches of the covenant.

The Creation of a Relational Covenant

We should recognize from the beginning that every community has many unexpressed and often conflicting rules as to how people should be treated. Being unexpressed, they provide no assistance in creating communal understanding and accountability. Being conflicting, they create more conflict. The development of a relational covenant for an organization involves bringing to expression a transparent, clear, and shared understanding by the community of what should be included in the covenant.

To be valued and valuable to a community, these covenants must grow out of the life of the community, express the vision, values, and strengths of the community, and be owned by the members of the community. Ground rules simply imposed on a community do not have the "buy in" that would make them covenants. They do not enter into the blood stream of the community. They do not become part of the culture of the community.

A relational covenant is the shared expectations and aspirations of a community or group as to how each member wants to be treated in the life of the community. A relational covenant becomes a set of promises to one another and to the community as a whole. Such covenants are more than rules about negative conduct and problems to be avoided; more than ways of bringing deviant conduct back into line. They are affirmations of the vision and values of the community and the positive conduct that expresses that vision and those values.

Relational covenants are, in the words of Kay Pranis, "shared values in action, expressed in a practical manner." First, this means the covenant grows out of our shared values and these values are going to guide our action. Second, these values, to guide our behavior, need to be expressed in a practical manner, in specific, not abstract, behavior that defines what the values look like in practice. Let's look at the circle covenant below as an example of what Kay means.

Covenant for a Circle Process

MAINTAIN CONFIDENTIALITY.
- *What is shared while in circle stays in circle.*
- *Personal information that is shared in circle is kept confidential except when safety would be compromised and except to the extent that the circle agrees on what is to be shared.*

SPEAK WITH RESPECT.
- *Speak only when you have the talking piece.*
- *Speak only for yourself.*
- *Speak from the heart.*
- *Be specific.*
- *Speak in a way that encourages dialogue.*
- *Be brief and to the point.*

LISTEN WITH RESPECT.
- *Listen for understanding.*
- *Be open to being transformed.*

STAY IN CIRCLE.
- *Respect for the circle calls upon people to stay in circle while the circle works to find resolution to the issues raised.*

Let's look at the section "Speak with respect" as an example. Yes, we should speak with respect. This is a key value and it is aspirational. What does such speaking look like in practice? Well, it means "to speak only when you hold the talking piece." This is something we can observe. It is practical. We can judge whether we and others are following this guideline in the covenant. If we start speaking for everyone we have talked with in the parking lot and on the Internet, we know and others will know that we are not following the covenant: "Speak only for yourself." If we start talking about a person's character and not specific conduct, we know and others will know that we have forgotten the covenant: "Be specific." If we start rambling on, we and others will know we are not being respectful of others' right to talk: "Be brief and to the point." Describing the value in terms of practical behavior is essential to our ability to know when we and others are not speaking respectfully. At the same time, we all have a sense of what is respectful and what is not, and we cannot practically list all behavior. I find that there is a dynamic relation between the value and our attempt to describe the value in a practical way, trying our best to define the behavior, but also relying on the value itself and our sense of what is respectful.

Covenants in Circles

The covenant above is a fairly typical covenant for a circle process. In my experience, most covenants address how we speak and listen as well as confidentiality. Confidentiality is critically important in providing the space that is safe enough for people in conflict to talk authentically. We need to maintain these confidences. The ideal is for the group to move to transparency, but this can only be done by agreement at the end of the process, where everyone agrees what should be said to the world outside the circle. I also like to include the provision about staying in circle until we all agree, or agree we have done all that we can under the circumstances.

As we prepare for the circle, we work together on the covenant. In circles that are meeting on a onetime basis, I generally offer the covenant above to encourage their thinking. I ask if there is anything they would subtract or add. Before the circle meets, I circulate the covenant as part of the agreement for the circle. When we come together in the circle, I make sure everyone still agrees with the relational covenant, asking again if there is anything that should be added or changed. We then sign the covenant together. The time spent on the covenant is an opportunity to find common ground before getting to the difficult discussions.

The covenant does change the tone and behavior of a circle. The conversation is still filled with truth and emotion, but the way it is expressed is more constructive than it otherwise would be. The covenant is self-regulating. I find people really do work to maintain it. The steward does have ultimate responsibility for seeing that the covenant is followed, but I have rarely needed to remind anyone of the covenant. When I do, I do so in the spirit that the breaking of the covenant was the result of old habits more than intentional disrespect. Any reminder of the covenant is done with soft hands, with a certain gentleness, not with anger or with the spirit of punishment.

Covenants in Our Ongoing Institutional Lives

A relational covenant is something every organization should create. There is nothing more important to prevent destructive conflict than such a covenant. These covenants again should arise out of the best and deepest values of the organization and should be expressed in a practical manner. I have worked, for example with local churches, with leadership teams, such as a bishop's cabinet, and with larger judicatory bodies, such as an annual conference in the United Methodist Church. Each of these organizations dealt with topics such as the following:

- How would you like to be treated in any meeting or decision-making process of the organization?
- How should members of the body of Christ be treated?
- How do we encourage respect for each member as a child of God?
- How do we create sanctuary or safety for each member of the community?
- How do we listen for understanding, speak the truth in love, use our imaginations, and be forgiving?
- How are we going to make decisions?
- How do we deal with the issues of confidentiality and transparency?
- How do we deal with accountability to the covenant?
- How do we maintain an openness to revise the covenant as needed?

As an example, here is one way an organization, such as a church, might develop such a covenant. Once you have gathered the circle of people who will be developing the relational covenant, whether that is the whole community or a group of leaders and representatives, begin the process with an exercise. Divide into groups, with three or four members in each group, two large sheets of paper, some markers, and scissors. Each member of the group answers these questions: When have we experienced our best moments in this community? When have we been most like the beloved community? Tell the stories. Then look at what values these stories share. List these common values on one sheet of paper that is visible to the group as they reflect on the next question.

Given the values we have listed, what specific behaviors reflect and promote our values and what behaviors do not? Each group is to write the desired behaviors inside a large circle that is drawn on the second sheet of paper, and to list unwanted behaviors outside the circle. Then, to deal with the unwanted behaviors, make sure there is a desired behavior included in the circle that would prevent or discourage each of the unwanted behaviors. Cut out the circle of desired behaviors, and discard the rest, or incorporate them later into a ritual of repentance.

Each group or a representative from each group will then share with the whole group their core values and desired behaviors. The first group will probably have the longest presentation as subsequent groups will only need to add any new values or behaviors that have not yet been mentioned. With each new item, check on agreement from the whole and discuss any concerns. Set aside on a separate sheet for further work any points that do not have full agreement.

The collection of values and desired behaviors is the raw material for the crafting of the community's relational covenant by a smaller group. Make sure everyone can see these lists or has a copy upon which they can reflect as you proceed to the next stage of development. Entrust to a small group the important task of integrating the list of core values and the corresponding list of desired behaviors into a working draft of the relational covenant that is then considered, improved, and approved by the whole community.

There are other ways to do this. Do the exercise in each of the committees in the church. Make sure you involve the youth, as they often have the best ideas. Then bring the result to the whole body to integrate, improve, and approve.

Whatever you do, celebrate the covenant once it is approved. Post it prominently throughout the spaces of the organization, and periodically review and renew the covenant.

Conclusion

To conclude this chapter on ritual and relational covenants, let me share an adaptation of the familiar story "The Rabbi's Gift."

> Once a church had fallen upon hard times. Only five members were left: the pastor and four others, all over sixty years old. In the mountains near the church there lived a retired rabbi. It occurred to the pastor to ask the rabbi if he could offer any advice that might save the church. The pastor and the rabbi spoke at length, but when asked for advice, the rabbi simply responded by saying, "I have no

advice to give. The only thing I can tell you is that the Messiah is one of you."

The pastor, returning to the church, told the church members what the rabbi had said. In the months that followed, the old church members pondered the words of the rabbi. "The Messiah is one of us?" they each asked themselves. As they thought about this possibility, they all began to treat each other with extraordinary respect on the off chance that one among them might be the Messiah. And on the off, off chance that they might be the Messiah, they also began to treat themselves with extraordinary care.

As time went by, people visiting the church noticed the aura of respect and gentle kindness that surrounded the five old members of the small church. Hardly knowing why, more people began to come back to the church. They began to bring their friends, and their friends brought more friends. Within a few years, the small church had once again become a thriving church, thanks to the rabbi's gift.

I believe that ritual and relational covenants are such a gift. Both will make a difference in the life of a circle dealing with conflict, or in an organization trying to be more like the beloved community. Both will help us treat ourselves and one another "with extraordinary care."

SEVEN

Finding the Positive Core
Appreciative Inquiry

Appreciate the life-giving waters.

❧

*Elicit stories of peak experiences, grace-filled moments,
and dreams of a preferred future.*

The previous chapter dealt with creating and defining the space of the circle through ritual and a relational covenant as the space where we can bring our conflicts, our raw emotions, our authentic selves to be constructive together. In the next three chapters we are going to reflect on the three most important movements within the conversation of this circle. The first movement, in most situations, is to share and build on the positive and best in all the parties—peak experiences, grace-filled moments, and dreams of a preferred future. This movement is informed by the field of *appreciative inquiry* (hereinafter, AI). Sometimes the first movement is so successful that we do not need to move to the second movement, the movement from positions to addressing interests and needs. My experience is that most often we do need to address the negative, the issues that created the conflict, trying to move beneath positions to addressing the interests and needs of the parties. This movement is informed by the field of *interest-based mediation.* The final movement is a movement necessary in most conflicted situations; it addresses the harm experienced by the parties. This movement is informed by the field of *restorative justice.*

I find in my practice that I generally need to use all three of these approaches in a conflicted situation. Although I like to start with appreciative inquiry and then move to interest-based mediation and restorative justice, I sequence the process in a way that meets the needs of the group and the flow of the conversation. As I said in the beginning of this book, the work of conflict transformation is improvisational.

In this chapter we will explore the lessons of AI and its most important activity—the asking of appreciative and powerful questions. We have talked about *creating a well together* and *experiencing the well as sacred relational space.* In this chapter, we are talking about *appreciating the abundant life-giving waters*, inviting persons to share from their own wells about what gives them life and letting these stories become the focus of the common well, a source of strength and guidance for everyone in the process. Here we talk about how we draw upon the deep, life-giving waters found in every person and in every human system. Ultimately, we want to drink deeply together of the abundant waters that can reconcile and heal and that truly quench our thirst. (See John 4:7-15.)

Appreciative Inquiry Stories

A company in Mexico was judged the worst place for women to work in the country. The company recognized the problem and tried to solve it through sensitivity training and through rules and regulations. The result of this problem solving was that the conditions became worse. The company then asked David Cooperrider of the Weatherhead School of Management of Case Western Reserve University, the founder of AI, to help. His approach was to inquire about men and women in the company who were working well together. The best of the company then became models for the whole company. They told their stories and the company built a culture around their stories. The company over time became the best place in Mexico for women to work.

I facilitated a conversation in the midst of a worship war in a church. Some members of the congregation liked Bach cantatas or a traditional service, and other members liked a contemporary service or what the traditionalists called "seven eleven music," seven words sung eleven times. Five representatives of each group comprised the circle. Instead of beginning with the problem or with what each group disliked about the other's way of worship, I asked each to reflect from their preference of worship on a time when they felt particularly close to God and neighbor. Half of the members of the circle, in telling their stories, were moved to tears by the memories. The stories were all remarkable and life-giving. After the last of the ten spoke, there was a universal affirmation that all ten wanted worship to include all that was contained in the stories. We never got to the discussion of the negative. The group then began to design worship that built on all these stories. The stories generated much energy for moving forward together.

Lessons of Appreciative Inquiry

The word *appreciate* means "valuing; the act of recognizing the best in people or the world around us; affirming past and present strengths, successes, and potentials; to perceive those things that give life (health, vitality, excellence) to living systems." Inquiry is "the act of exploration and discovery . . . to ask questions."[1]

AI is a philosophy of positive change and a methodology for discovering and building on the positive core of any human system. "At the heart of AI is the understanding that human systems move in the direction of what they continuously study, analyze, and discuss. AI is therefore a call to study 'root causes of success,' rather than 'root causes of failure.'" Carl Jung at the end of his career stated that "he had never seen people grow *from* a problem. Instead, he suggested, they grow *toward* some more compelling life force."[2]

Appreciative inquiry begins with the assumption that all human systems have something to value in the present or in their past. Together parties to these systems then search for what is valued, the best. This search involves appreciative questions aimed at *discovering* this "positive core." AI then works to change the system through *dreaming* about what might be if the system were based on this positive core, *designing* or constructing the system so that it promotes the positive core, and then living out this *destiny* through inspired action that works to fulfill the dream and the design. AI describes these four steps as the "4-D Cycle": Discovery, Dream, Design, and Destiny or Delivery. This process involves the members of the whole system, not just the leaders. AI is about collaborative transformation.

Think about how this approach might help us as we work to create positive change in the church. This approach is different from our usual problem-solving approach, looking at the problems, at the negative and trying to figure out how to solve the problems—for example, declining numbers, declining giving, increasing conflicts, losing the youth. With this focus, we often find ourselves even more stuck in the problems. The problem is often a small part of the overall picture, but it overwhelms our ability to see other aspects of the person or institution or situation.

AI recognizes that every church, no matter how troubled, has had good moments. People would not be in the church if things were all bad. Start from the positive, from people's best moments, their peak experiences, their grace-filled moments, instead of from the negative or the problems. Focusing on strengths is more effective than focusing on problems. And it is more constructive to build on what is known and appreciated in the system than trying to imagine an abstract ideal of a better self or a better community.

For me, this starting point is theologically sound because it grows out of a theology of abundance instead of a theology of scarcity. Jesus says, "I came that they may have life, and have it abundantly" (John 10:10). This approach affirms that everyone has a positive core as a child of God, created in the image of God, with glimmers of the divine, even those who have done very negative things. This approach has an appreciative view of creation, which God says is "very good." Even people who see only a fallen creation respond better when asked about the "best" rather than about the "worst." This positive approach is consistent with our understanding of the need for a positive attitude about the purposes and potentials of conflict—an attitude that sees conflict as natural and necessary: a resource for learning, growth, and revelation. This positive approach also supports our assertion that in conflict we can be well and be a well, that we can create safe and sacred space through rituals and relational covenants, and that people can find empowerment and recognition. The collaborative nature of this venture is affirmative of the importance of relationship and the power of people to create their own preferred future.

Yes, even when we affirm that creation is good, very good, as God says in Genesis, we must recognize that life is not always what it was created to be. In many situations, we need to name this reality, inquire about it and engage the problem, engage the harm, engage the brokenness. This we will address in the next two chapters. The AI approach to change and to conflict transformation is a very powerful and important first step in most situations. I like the transformation that occurs, for example, in the story of the Mexican company, when the negative problem of sexual harassment was reframed by looking at positive male-female working relationships. I like the process of helping others try to find the positive in each other, not just the negative. In the context of such positive stories, problems can then be addressed more easily and constructively. Most importantly, I believe in the power of the appreciative question in the context of conflicted situations.

The Role and Power of Questions

The Importance of Questions

According to T. S. Eliot, "Jesus is one who knows how to ask questions."[3] Much of what Jesus says is in the form of a question. "Someone in the crowd said to him, 'Teacher, tell my brother to divide the family inheritance with me.' But he said to him, 'Friend, who set me to be a judge or arbitrator over you?'" (Luke 12:13-14) Here Jesus is acting like a good mediator, refusing to judge or arbitrate. His question puts the matter back in the hands of the family.

Jesus teaches us the importance of questions—questions that open up new ways of thinking and living. In fact, I have come to believe that one of the primary roles of a leader, including the role of the steward of a circle, is to ask good questions. We often think that a leader should give the answers, that a mediator should give us the solution to our problem. What an impossible burden! Moreover, when we are honest, do we really have the answer, the answer that will work for the community or for the participants in a conflict?

Peter Storey was the Presiding Bishop for the Methodist Church in Southern Africa when Nelson Mandela was freed from prison and South Africa was being freed from apartheid. He chaired a planning group for a convocation called 'The Journey to a New Land' which was designed to prepare the church for a new, transformed South Africa. After months of planning and the finalizing of a program, a survey of the thirteen districts across Southern Africa revealed a poor response. Few people seemed interested. The Black Methodist Consultation (BMC) gave it a thumbs-down, not because they opposed the gathering but because they questioned the *process* through which it was coming about. Their message was blunt: "If our people are to really own what comes out of this, stop planning from the top-down. Let the people themselves write the agenda—then it will be their journey."

Peter Storey and his committee heard the message and started over, asking the members of each district to submit their concerns to the committee. The momentum began to gather and before July of 1993, some fourteen thousand submissions had flooded into the *Journey* offices! A deep reservoir of concern had been tapped, the people were heard, and the people participated.[4]

Rainer Maria Rilke has helped me understand the importance of questions and the power of living with the questions. He says:

> Have patience with everything that remains unsolved in your heart. Try to love the *questions themselves*, like locked rooms and like books written in a foreign language. Do not now look for the answers. They cannot now be given to you because you could not live them. It is a question of experiencing everything. At present you need to *live* the questions.[5]

For me, living the question is more about finding inspiration than answers. For me this is consistent with what Jung said about growing not from a problem but from a more compelling life force.

Elie Wiesel takes the asking of questions to a higher level in the book *Night*, his memoir about the Holocaust. As a young man, his spiritual master, Moshe, tells him that every question possesses a power that does not lie in its answer. "Man raises himself toward God by the questions he asks Him," Moshe explains. Moshe adds that he cannot understand God's answers. Wiesel then asks Moshe why, then, does he pray. Moshe replies: "I pray to the God within me that He will give me the strength to ask Him the right questions."[6] Whether I am asking questions of God or of participants in a circle, my prayer is that I ask the right questions.

One of the major concepts of AI is that groups move in the direction of the questions they ask. The kinds of questions people ask determines what they will find, and what they find then sets the directions for the journey toward change. Another principle of AI is that the seeds of change are embedded in the questions we ask. These concepts give real importance to the question and to the person who is framing the question. This power is something that cannot be taken lightly.

The Example of the Quaker Clearness Committee

My friend Elise Boulding taught me about a process known as the Quaker clearness committee, a forum where people can bring their dilemmas, their problems, in order to seek greater clarity. When she was deciding whether to marry Kenneth Boulding, she and Kenneth asked for a group of wise people in the Meeting of Friends to help them gain clarity on what they should do. The role of the wise people was not to give advice, make judgments, or tell them what to do. They simply asked honest, open questions that assisted Elise and Kenneth in finding their own answers and to reaching their own decision.

In *Let Your Life Speak,* Parker Palmer describes how a clearness committee helped him decide whether to be a president of a college.[7] At first the questions were easy, he reports, concerning, for example, his vision for the institution. Then he was asked, "What would you like most about being a president?" This question moved him from his head to his heart, and he unleashed a series of responses as to what he would *not* like about the job. The person who had posed the question noted that he had asked what he would *like* about the job. The only answer Palmer was able to give, an answer that appalled even him, was that he would get his picture in the paper with the word *president* underneath. After a long, respectful silence someone asked whether there were an easier way to get his picture in the paper. Palmer realized that if he took the job it would have been bad for him and a disaster for the school.

For me, the clearness committee models what the steward of a circle can do: asking powerful questions that open up the head and the heart, prompting participants to explore their assumptions and values. This approach will help them gain greater clarity on how to get to a better place together.

Questions in Circles

An important role of the steward is to ask powerful questions: questions that get at the positive core; questions that elicit stories and the affirmative aspects of everyone's story; questions that take the group to deeper levels and new ideas.

The most powerful tool we have is an open-ended, positive question. My first question is often "What are your hopes for our time together?" The first question is not "What are the problems that have brought you here?" A follow-up question might be "If your hopes for our meeting are fulfilled, what will your relationships look like?" In the sacred space of conflict, remembering grace-filled moments and expressing dreams of a preferred future, the primary question is always: What is God's love calling us to be and to do?

These questions must come out of real curiosity and a desire to understand and learn. They should never be rhetorical questions. These questions express genuine care and wonder. I have found that whenever I am tempted to go beyond a summary of their responses and tell them what to do, I am always well served to turn whatever statement I was thinking of making into a question.

Our questions must also allow people to dream. Sharing dreams and hopes together can reveal strong preferences, deep values and desires. People in conflict often find points of connection when sharing dreams of a preferred future that builds on their stories. Dreaming inspires creativity and innovation, thinking "out of the box."

We need to take the time and care to craft these questions. In my preparation, I work hard at the questions I will ask. I make sure they speak to the unique context of the conflict with which I am engaged. I then let go of all but two or three questions, so I can follow the responses with questions that relate to what has been said. I generally do start with a question that gets at the hopes of the participants and a second question that gets at their stories.

Another approach I have used with large groups is to inquire about their best moments in community and then ask what in the life of the community is getting in the way of a fuller experience of this positive core.

Conclusion

The lessons of AI are important in our work to transform conflict. Sharing stories of peak experiences and dreams of a preferred future may serve to resolve the presenting problem in a group. At least, perhaps, participants will see the issue in a larger context. But when the original problem or problems persist, the group needs to address them. Having shared the positive, people can now more readily address the negative. Sometimes the conflict is so emotional that we must start with the problem and then later move to the positive core or grace-filled stories. How do we do this? We now turn to the lessons learned from interest-based mediation and then to the lessons learned from restorative justice.

EIGHT

Meeting Needs
Interest-Based Mediation

Go beneath the surface.

∽◎∾

Move from positions to interests and needs,
generating options to reach consensus.

A "problem" is an issue such as a dispute over worship styles in which one group takes the position that they want contemporary music and the other takes the position that they want traditional music. We should note that such disputes usually include issues of harm, which are addressed in the next chapter. For interest-based mediation, a focus on problems involves moving from *positions* to *interests and needs*, generating options, evaluating options, and reaching consensus on an agreement. This methodology was developed in a book published in 1981 entitled *Getting to Yes: Negotiating Agreement Without Giving In*, by Roger Fisher and William Ury. The goal of this method is a wise agreement "defined as one that meets the legitimate interests of each side to the extent possible, resolves conflicting interests fairly, is durable, and takes community interests into account." In reaching this goal, there were two other criteria:

efficiency and improvement of the relationship, at least no damage to the relationship.[1] We will explore this methodology and conclude with a discussion of the Jerusalem Council described in Acts 15:1-29.

The Problem with Positions

Most people enter into discussions around conflicts talking primarily in terms of their positions or demands: "I want the minister to stay." "I want the minister to leave." Criticizing people or their positions or trying to get parties to compromise and "back off" from their demands generally causes them to cling more stubbornly to them. Focusing on positions leads to impasse, sometimes compromise, but rarely to creative solutions that meet everyone's needs and interests. Positions are statements or demands framed as solutions. They express a solution to deep needs and interests. Interests and needs motivate people to take positions. Positions often obscure what parties really want. The presenting issue in a conflict is often not the most important issue for the parties. A fight in a marriage over the checkbook often signifies deeper issues about trust and power.

The good news is that a position usually represents just one possible solution to the needs and interests of the parties. Knowing this, instead of focusing on positions, we can help the parties verbalize underlying interests and needs and find common solutions to these interests and needs. The other good news is that, although needs and interests may conflict, shared and compatible ones can be discovered. Different interests can create opportunities as well.

Move from Positions to Interest and Needs

Rather than challenging the demands people put forward, as the facilitator you move the discussion to the underlying interests or needs. This begins by seeking more information through open-ended questions that draw out these underlying needs and interests. "Why do you want to control the checkbook?" "Why do you want the minister to leave or stay?" "What do you see as your most important needs?" This is a critical transition that must take place in order for people to begin to work together to resolve the issues on which there is conflict.

An example often used is the story of two children arguing over an orange. The position of each child was that they wanted the orange. If one child gets the orange, then the other child loses. The loser does not think this is a wise agreement and the relationship has not been improved. If someone plays Solomon and splits the orange in two, a compromise has been reached, but no one is fully satisfied and, as you shall see, there is a lost opportunity. At the heart of the alternative to positional negotiation is getting beneath the positions to find out why each child wants the orange. Asking the question, we discover one child wants the orange for the juice and the other wants the peel in order to make a pie. Knowing this, both parties can get all they want—their interests can be met by what is described as a win/win agreement, and the relationship is sustained.

In this process the parties discover there are many compatible and shared interests and needs. We all have, for example, basic human needs, including security, economic well-being, a sense of belonging, recognition, some control over one's life. Once you recognize and agree on meeting the shared interests, the conflicting ones are more manageable. Parties usually have several interests. The more interests that are surfaced, the more options you can generate for meeting at least some of the interests. Some interests are more important than others. This process allows for setting priorities as to which are most important. Relatively minor ones might be part of a compromise when the major ones are met.

Generate and Evaluate Options to Meet These Needs and Interests

Once the interests and needs are known, the most creative part of the process begins—generating options to meet these interests and needs. Newsprint, which can be posted on the wall, and an easel are the two essential props in most facilitations. As you go through the process of storytelling and then working to understand needs and interests, you will list these interests and needs on the newsprint without preference or priority. Before moving to try to meet these interests or needs, ask if there is anything not listed, any other issues to be considered. Give people time to think; this is the time to state all concerns. You do not want to work out an agreement and then discover significant issues have not been discussed. Once everyone has agreed on the list of concerns to be addressed, you can begin the process of seeking options for meeting the interests and needs of all the parties.

You may, as I often find, have several sheets filled with interests and needs. The parties look at this list and wonder where to start. You can lead a process of organizing the interests and needs, finding that they generally group into a few issues that become manageable. I often take a break at this point and do my best to organize the issues into categories. I then list the issues on newsprint in the order I would like to address them.

When the group comes back together, make sure everyone agrees with the organization and wording of the issues. Now start to work on one issue at a time. I usually start with the easiest one to resolve. We have already talked about brainstorming in chapter 3 where we dealt with the imagination. Here you brainstorm as many ideas as possible, without critical evaluation. Encourage everyone to turn off their censors and let the ideas flow. This is where it gets exciting! Ideas are generated or discovered that no one had thought of when they entered the room. You never know who will express the best idea. Welcome every idea and list them all without comment.

Once the group has exhausted its ideas, move to evaluating the pros and cons of the options to determine which ones best meet the interests and needs of the parties. In large groups, you could give each person two or three adhesive dots or stars to put beside his or her favorite ideas. You will then see fairly quickly the most productive ideas to evaluate and to improve. In smaller groups, simply ask people to talk about their favorite idea or their preferences. The best part of this process is when people begin to improve the preferred or favorite ideas, making them even better.

Proceed to the next issue and follow the same process. Throughout the whole process of storytelling, moving to interests and needs, and generating options, look for opportunities to point out areas of commonality and positive intentions. Affirm constructive moves and highlight progress in order to continue to develop momentum to an agreement on all the issues.

Tools for Breaking Impasse

Sometimes all flows smoothly through an appreciative process and/or through positions to interest and needs to consensus. At other times, in deeply conflicted situations, the journey is more like a roller coaster ride. The situation may seem especially bleak just before a breakthrough. The circle has hit a wall. How do you break through in those tough moments? Here are some tools.

The first is use of caucuses, separate meetings with the parties. In these caucuses, the parties will open up and talk more freely. Begin to explore their ideas for breaking the impasse. Do this with all the parties.

You may need to work between them for a period of time until you judge that it would be fruitful to bring people back together. In the caucuses, do reality checks. What will happen if they don't agree? What are the costs and benefits of agreeing or not agreeing? What is the worst-case scenario if people do not reach an agreement?

Often in these caucuses I also look for objective criteria on which all parties might agree, like the law, what a court might do, professional standards, expert opinions, even how the Bible could suggest criteria on which parties could agree. All this is done in a noncoercive way, but these criteria outside the positions of the parties can be useful.

Sometimes I just acknowledge to a group that we seem to be stuck and let the circle take responsibility for it. A moment of silence may prompt someone to come forward with a suggestion. A moment of prayer can remind everyone that we are not alone. Often I will suggest taking a break for a walk during which everyone reflects on how we can break the impasse. I am always amazed at the constructive ideas that come out after a walk. Sometimes we need to take a break for the evening; everyone rests with the issues and prayerfully discerns what God's love is leading us to do. I never forget the mantra: trust God, trust yourself, trust the wisdom of others, and trust the process.

Write Up the Agreement

Once the group does reach consensus, write up the agreement. This agreement should summarize the consensus, including specifics—who, what, when, where, how. Be clear. Check with everyone to make sure it is realistic. Discuss and agree on how to handle any further problems that arise—ideally, agreeing to return to the circle. Make sure everything is included in the agreement. Have the parties sign and date the agreement.

If issues remain on which there is no agreement, state what progress has been made and agree on a process for continuing to deal with those issues.

Conclusion

Then certain individuals came down from Judea and were teaching the brothers, "Unless you are circumcised according to the custom of Moses, you cannot be saved." And after Paul and Barnabas had no small dissension and debate with them, Paul and Barnabas and some of the others were appointed to go up to Jerusalem to discuss this question with the apostles and the elders. . . . The apostles and the elders met together to consider this matter. . . . The whole assembly kept silence, and listened. ". . . we have decided unanimously to choose representatives and send them to you. . . . For it has seemed good to the Holy Spirit and to us to impose on you no further burden than these essentials: that you abstain from what has been sacrificed to idols and from blood and from what is strangled and from fornication. If you keep yourselves from these, you will do well." (Acts 15:1-29)

I know of no better summary of the interest-based mediation from start to finish than the events described in Acts 15. We can also see elements of an appreciative inquiry as well. Paul and Barnabas have been traveling in foreign territories and sharing the good news of Jesus to the Gentiles. They receive dramatic responses. They then return to the sending church in Antioch of Syria. They call the church together and relate "all that God had done with them, and how [God had] opened a door of faith for the Gentiles" (Acts 14:27-28). Then some folks arrive from Judea and preach to the Gentile believers that unless they "are circumcised according to the custom of Moses," they "cannot be saved" (15:1). Paul and Barnabas and some of the others were appointed to go up to Jerusalem to discuss this question with the apostles and the elders. This sets the stage for what some call the Jerusalem Council. What can we learn from what happens in Jerusalem? The issues are significant to us as Gentiles: we are now included in the covenant as a result of the decisions made at this council. There were two issues, with important underlying interests and needs:

The first was circumcision. Did you need to become a Jew to become a Christian? We need to give the folks from Judea their due, as we should in any discussion of a controversial issue. They were sincere men. They understood that circumcision was the cornerstone of their understanding of the Law. They were concerned that if circumcision goes, the Law goes. Their deepest interest was preserving the place and importance of the Law. The Law held people together in spite of exile and foreign occupation. The Law gave them the character to resist the culture of idolatry and lack of neighborliness.

The second issue was social intercourse. Here the focus is on Jewish and Gentile Christians eating together at the same table, with significant issues around what is clean and unclean. In some ways, social intercourse was a more serious issue because it was at the common meals that religious fellowship found its deepest expression.

There was "no small dissension and debate" (Acts 15:2). Might this be an understatement? They did not shy away from the conflict. Paul and Barnabas took a long journey to get together with the key people to make a communal decision. They all had the courage to come together to discuss their conflict. They demonstrated how conflict is an opportunity for growth, learning, and revelation.

The participants in the Jerusalem Council named and defined the conflict. They created the space and the time for all voices to be heard, for the stories to be told. We can learn something from each of the conversations at the Jerusalem Council.

"After there had been much debate," Peter speaks out of his own experience with Cornelius and his vision of the large sheet coming down from heaven with four-footed animals, beasts of prey, reptiles, and birds of the air and the voice that said, "What God has made clean, you must not call profane" (Acts 10:9-16). Peter notes that God has made "no distinction between them and us," and asks why they need to burden Gentiles with the yoke of observance which Jews themselves had found too heavy to bear. We are "saved through the grace of the Lord Jesus" (Acts 15:7-11). Peter had the courage to stand up and not fear as he did in Antioch, when he backed off from eating with the Gentiles "for fear of the circumcision faction" (Gal. 2:12).

Paul and Barnabas bear witness to the evident blessing of God upon their own mission to the Gentiles. They did not argue. They simply told of the good works of God with the Gentiles (Acts 15:12). This testimony appears to be the most effective of all the approaches.

James then speaks and says that Peter's relation with Cornelius is in keeping with scripture. He uses scripture to affirm the new direction, which is contrary to other scripture (vv. 13-21).

"The whole assembly kept silence" (v. 12). They listened deeply. The assembly and the leaders were open to discern what God was revealing to them. They then came to a consensus, the "consent of the whole church," "unanimously" (vv. 22, 25). They came to a decision that attempted to address the needs of everyone: there would be no further burden of circumcision, and they recognized the "essentials" of the law, summed up in no food sacrificed to idols (no idolatry), and no fornication (no offenses against neighborliness).

The Jerusalem Council is the model for holy conferencing in the church. The Jerusalem Council teaches us the importance of getting together to address our positions, our issues, our problems; having the courage to name them and address the interests and needs of each side; telling and listening to the stories; being open to discern what God was revealing to them through these stories; and affirming that people can come to consensus in a way that meets the important interests and needs of all. Remarkable! This book is written in the belief and the experience that we can have such conversations today.

Now let us turn to the third movement in the circle conversation, addressing the harm that has been created and the lessons learned from restorative justice.

NINE

Addressing Harm

Restorative Justice

Drink deeply the healing waters.

*Move from retribution to restoration:
healing the harm, affirming accountability,
and creating a new relationship.*

A Lawyer's Story

On the first day of my practice as a lawyer, I found an audiotape from my new boss waiting for me. He was out of the office on a month-long trial. On the tape, he described the work he wanted me to do while he was gone and also gave me some practical advice about trial practice. He then went on to describe each of the partners in the firm, explaining their different styles. For example, he described one of the Catholic partners who attended Mass every morning as a feisty, aggressive slugger. He described the partner who was a Quaker as the greatest gentleman he had ever known, soft-spoken and kind. On cross-examination, the feisty, aggressive lawyer would feint and then punch and bludgeon the witness to a bloody pulp. The witness would see the blows coming, but there was nothing the witness could do about it. On the other hand, the Quaker was different. He used a stiletto. Because of the soft-spoken nature of the Quaker, the witness would generally never see the stiletto coming and would sometimes not even know when it entered between the ribs. The result, my boss concluded, was the same with both approaches. After the cross-examination there was a pool of blood under the witness chair.

Wasn't my boss being honest about the process? Even when you want to do it differently, doesn't an adversarial retributive system tend toward blood under the chair? Over the course of my practice, I found that the adversarial process increases animosity and estrangement. Everyone is wounded. The goal is to win, but many people come away from litigation feeling that everyone has lost, and that the lawyers are the only ones who benefit from the process. Truth also loses. People justify lies and deceit. In fact, my experience with the adversarial retributive system is that its emphasis on winning, with painful consequences for losing, creates an atmosphere for lying, denial, and self-justification.

In the courtroom, there is no real opportunity for empathy and recognition or apology and forgiveness. There is no real encounter or dialogue between the parties. The system does not work to heal people or relationships. Lawsuits almost always exacerbate anger, wounds, divisions, greed, and desire for revenge. The financial and emotional costs are immense. Is this the justice people want or deserve? Perhaps this is why law professors and the legal community are so reluctant to talk about justice.

The Importance of Justice to God

In the book of Amos, God says:

> "I hate, I despise your festivals,
> and I take no delight in your solemn assemblies. . . .
> Take away from me the noise of your songs;
> I will not listen to the melody of your harps.
> But let justice roll down like waters,
> and righteousness like an ever-flowing stream." (Amos 5:21, 23-24)

Justice is more important to God than worship. The worth of worship is contingent upon being just and righteous in one's relationships, fulfilling the demands of relationships. Abraham Heschel, the Jewish theologian, in his book *The Prophets* asks, "Why should religion, the essence of which is worship of God, put such stress on justice . . . ?" Heschel approaches this question by looking at the partnership of God and humanity in the creation of history. God needs humans to help in accomplishing God's "grand design."[1]

Earlier we observed how the Bible moves from unlimited retribution in the law of Lamech in Genesis 4:24 ("seventy-sevenfold"), to an eye for an eye, to unlimited forgiveness ("seventy-seven times" in Matthew 18:22). We see the justice God seeks is ultimately not retributive. What is the justice God desires?

A Search for a Better Understanding of Justice

In my search for a better understanding of justice, I have not concluded that there is no place for the adversarial retributive system. There are cases that need to be tried, both because of precedent-setting issues and because in some cases the parties are not able to resolve their disputes. We need strong advocates, a noble role. I affirm the primary value of retributive justice, which is the affirmation that we are moral agents who should be held accountable and responsible for our actions. This is a moral universe! However, I am convinced that restorative justice includes an understanding not only of human beings as moral agents but also, for example, the value of the rule of law and the role of deterrence. For me, restorative justice puts these values in a more profound context, with its understanding of the importance of personal accountability.

The concept of restorative justice became much clearer to me when I studied the Truth and Reconciliation Commission in South Africa (hereinafter the TRC). Critics of the TRC asked, "Where is justice?" "Where are the adversarial retributive trials such as were experienced at Nuremberg after World War II in Germany?" I listened to Bishop Tutu agree that retributive justice was not the justice the Truth and Reconciliation Commission was seeking. There was another form of justice, restorative justice, which was consistent with the desire to seek truth and reconciliation. The final clause on National Unity and Reconciliation in the Interim Constitution of 1993 says this well:

> The pursuit of national unity, the well-being of all South African citizens and peace require reconciliation between the people of South Africa and the reconstruction of society. . . . There is a need for understanding but not revenge, a need for reparation but not for retaliation, a need for *ubuntu* but not for victimization.[2]

Upon my return from South Africa, I studied with Howard Zehr at Eastern Mennonite University. Much of what I say about restorative justice I learned from Howard, often called the father of the modern-day restorative justice movement. It has been gratifying to see how his understanding of justice is speaking to others, such as members of the board of the *Journal of Law and Religion*, with which I have been associated for the last twenty-five years, and to my friend Elise Boulding, who has spent her life working for peace. Upon discovering restorative justice, she said to me, "Tom, why hasn't anyone ever told me about this before now? This should be at the heart of peacebuilding." In her eighties, Elise started working on restorative justice initiatives. For me, restorative justice has become a way of life that allows us to *drink deeply the healing waters.*

A Comparison of Retributive and Restorative Justice

The following chart shows some of the differences between retributive and restorative justice: how each defines crime or wrongdoing, the aim of justice, and the process of justice. As I have noted earlier, this understanding of retributive justice informs more than just the criminal justice system. It has informed our way of dealing with grievances in the church through church trials, and it informs much of our way of dealing with conflicts in the world.

	RETRIBUTIVE JUSTICE	RESTORATIVE JUSTICE
CRIME OR WRONG-DOING	▪violation of the law ▪state is the victim	▪violation or harm to people/relationships in community
THE AIM OF JUSTICE	▪establish blame, guilt or liability ▪administer pain/ punishment	▪identify needs ▪identify obligations ▪promote healing
THE PROCESS OF JUSTICE	▪conflict between adversaries ▪winners and losers	▪collaborative engagement ▪maximizing information, dialogue and mutual agreement

Adapted from Howard Zehr

Retributive justice defines crime or wrongdoing as violation of the law. The question is whether the defendant broke the law, and, if so, how is he/she going to be punished. The focus is on the offender, not on the people who have been harmed. The law assists us in understanding when someone is harmed. However, the harm is harm to a person. Jesus says, "The sabbath was made for humankind, and not humankind for the sabbath" (Mark 2:27). The law was made for men and women, not men and women for the law. Restorative justice poses a different essential question: who has been harmed and how have they been harmed?

While retributive justice regards the state as the victim rather than the person or person directly harmed by the wrongdoing, restorative justice sees the harm in terms of people, relationships, and community. My experience is the person harmed is often harmed twice, once by the wrongdoing and then by the trial process, including cross-examination, where the person is seen primarily as a witness for the state. Restorative justice says we must start with the person harmed and then ask what the harm was to the community as a whole.

The aim of retributive justice is to establish blame, guilt, or liability. The aim of restorative justice is to identify the needs of the person harmed and to determine the obligations of the offender—and even the community—in addressing these harms. Instead of a punishment system, restorative justice creates an accountability system. What does the offender need to do personally to address the needs of the person harmed, to make things right? We are talking about real accountability to the victim. In the retributive system, third parties determine the punishment. This is coerced accountability, and, in my experience, the third-party punishment does not lead, in most cases, to acceptance of responsibility and to actions on the part of the offender personally to address the harms created. Punishment is often counterproductive to such accountability as it discourages empathy and encourages denial of responsibility. Punishment stigmatizes through shame, and shame is a primary cause of violence. Most people in prison see themselves as victims, and in many ways they are. In fact, their crimes often come out of their own victimhood; the punishment system adds to this sense of victimhood.

Restorative justice is able to see the offender in context, but, more importantly, gives the offender the chance to take personal responsibility for the actions that harmed another human being—to make things right. For some offenders, this accountability might involve the need for restraint. Zacchaeus is a biblical example of such accountability. He agrees to give half of his possessions to the poor and to restore fourfold to anyone whom he defrauded. Jesus' response to Zacchaeus was to tell him, "Today salvation has come to this house" (Luke 19:9).

The process of justice also differs in the two systems. Retributive justice is served by an adversarial process; restorative justice is served by a collaborative process. The latter process involves victims, offenders, and the community engaging one another with the goal of identifying obligations and solutions and promoting healing among the parties. This engagement ideally is direct, but sometimes it is indirect. In some cultures, a direct engagement would be inappropriate. An indirect engagement might involve a letter, an exchange of videos, or a surrogate.

Christopher Marshall articulates well the need for engagement of both parties: "Because they are bound together to the event, both victim and offender need each other to experience liberation and healing from the continuing thrall of the offense. The offender needs the victim to trigger or sharpen his contrition, to hear his confession, remit his guilt, and to affirm his ability to start fresh. The victim needs the offender to hear her pain, answer her questions, absorb her resentment, and affirm her dignity. Each holds the key to the other's liberation."[3]

In restorative justice the community is involved in working to heal the harm and support real accountability. The community recognizes its role in the harm as well. The community, a community of care, works to restore both the victim and the offender to the community. Restorative justice is about creating community.

Three words sum up restorative justice: *harm, accountability, engagement*. Restorative justice addresses victims' harms and needs, holds offenders accountable to make things right, and engages the victims, offenders, and communities in the process.

The Needs of the Parties

Another way to understand restorative justice is to look at the needs of each party: the person harmed, the one who harmed, and the community. As a preface to this discussion, we should note that in many cases we find ourselves as both victims and offenders, and we should also remember that only the parties can truly describe their needs, and different people have different needs. However, as I have listened to parties to a wrongdoing, the needs described below are mentioned over and over again.

Needs of Those Harmed

Victimization leads to disorder, disempowerment, and disconnection. The journey toward healing involves finding order, empowerment, and new relational connections. Finding order involves *safety*. The person harmed ideally needs to know that he or she will not be harmed again. Finding empowerment involves *being heard*, *finding answers*, and vindication through *restitution* and *accountability*, and through *participation*. This experience is the experience of recovering some control over one's life. Finding new relational connections involves a journey of *healing*.

The victim needs to be able to tell his or her story without interruption with all the feelings, in a space where people truly listen, understand, and acknowledge the harm. Repeating the story numerous times often serves a therapeutic purpose, providing a way to re-story one's life. Telling the story to the offender offers an opportunity to have the offender understand how the victim has been harmed.

In response to the telling of the story, a victim needs to receive answers. What really happened? Why me? Why you? What has happened since? A victim generally does not get this kind of information through the legally restrained procedures of the courtroom. The victim is left to speculate. Only the offender can really answer these questions.

The harm needs to be addressed. There needs to be accountability that addresses actual losses and has symbolic value. The accepting of responsibility conveys the message that the victim is not to be blamed. At the heart of accountability is the experience of vindication by the victim. Apologies are an important part of such vindication and accountability.

The victim needs to participate: telling the story, naming the harm, and deciding what needs to be done to address the harm. This involvement is critical to a sense of empowerment. Meeting all these needs is a way toward removing shame and humiliation—toward healing.

Needs of the Offender

I am often surprised that offenders do not fully *understand the harm* they have done until they actually hear the victim describe the harm. They need to know so they can respond with real accountability. Yes, most people experience guilt, even if it is not verbalized, and need to *cope with this guilt*. Every person needs to be *seen in context* as he or she is more than what is seen in the moment of the crime. Offenders are most often victims and their crimes come out of a sense of shame. James Gilligan, New York University professor and former prison psychiatrist, says,

"The emotion of shame is the primary or ultimate cause of all violence, whether toward others or toward the self."[4] The processes of restorative justice allow everyone to get to know the full history and personhood of the offender. To be personally accountable, the offender needs to *share in the decision* about what he or she will do to *make things right*. Ultimately, the offender needs to be *reintegrated into community*, one of our greatest needs, and experience transformation and *healing*. This journey will often involve treatment, personal growth, and sometimes restraint, at least temporarily.

Needs of the Community

When the state becomes the victim, our sense of community and our understanding of our responsibilities in community diminishes. The community is also impacted by crime. *Safety* is important to us. As community members we also have responsibilities. The community needs to *support and assist those harmed*, something we often find hard to do. We also need to hold offenders accountable as well as work to *support, assist, and reintegrate offenders in the community*. Restorative justice processes, unlike a jury in a criminal case, provide the community the opportunity to think about its role in the wrongdoing and what can be done to *address the larger systemic issues* that led to the crime—the root causes. This activity is critical to the *healing* of the community.

Mennonites, for example, have developed circles of healing and accountability for sex offenders coming out of prison. These circles work with the community, affirming that they are going to do everything in their power to make sure the ex-offender does not offend again. These circles work with the offender to find a job and housing—a place in the community. They also help the offender on the journey of self-knowledge, of restraint and growth toward transformation. The exceptional work of these circles is a powerful story of "accompaniment," as described earlier in this book.

Involvement by community members is a gift to each of them as well. At a dinner meeting I found myself sitting beside a university chaplain who did not know my interest in restorative justice. He told me about his father, whom he described as a hard-bitten business man. He claimed he had never seen his father cry. His father had just called to tell him about his involvement in a circle process at a juvenile court where he and other church members listened to the victim and offender, helping to determine what the young offender needed to do to make things right. He said that when the talking piece came to him to talk, he started to cry. He was touched personally in places he did not know he was hurting.

Restorative Practices

Howard Zehr emphasizes keeping focus on the five principles of restorative justice as we develop practices:

1. Focus on the harms and consequent needs of the victims, as well as the communities' and the offenders';
2. Address the obligations that result from those harms (the obligations of the offenders, as well as the communities, and society's);
3. Use inclusive, collaborative processes;
4. Involve those with a legitimate stake in the situation, including victims, offenders, community members, and society;
5. Seek to put right the wrongs.[5]

Zehr goes on to say that these principles are rooted in the values that come out of the vision of interconnectedness and the understanding that harm to one is harm to all. This is balanced by an appreciation for our particularity, which "reminds us that context, culture, and personality are all important." For him, the values of restorative justice can be summed up in one word: "respect: respect for all, even those who are different from us, even those who seem to be our enemies. . . . If we pursue justice as respect, we will do justice restoratively."[6]

With these principles in mind, we will examine the three main practices of restorative justice. Participation in all of these is voluntary. The offender acknowledges, at least to some degree, his or her responsibility.

Victim Offender Conferences

The initiation of the modern restorative justice movement is usually located in Elmira, Ontario, in 1974. Two young men pleaded guilty to vandalizing twenty-two properties. David Worth and Mark Yantzi, two Mennonites involved with the court, suggested to the judge that the offenders meet the victims and do restitution. The judge first rejected this idea and then later ordered it. The four of them went door to door, meeting the residents and doing restitution. Out of this came the Victim Offender Reconciliation Program that has developed into Victim Offender Conferences. These conferences involve primarily the victim and the offender. They are worked with individually, and, when ready, are brought together by a facilitator to work out a restitution agreement. Others can participate, but they are in secondary roles.

Family Group Conference

The Family Group Conference (FGC) grew out of traditional Maori practices.[7] In 1989 the juvenile justice system of New Zealand was revolutionized so that the primary response to juvenile crime was the FGC, with the court system as a backup. A key focus of the FGC is to get young offenders to take responsibility for and change their behavior. The participants in the process here include family members, especially the family of the offender, other individuals significant to the parties, and justice officials. The victims are given the opportunity to tell their stories. At some point in the process, there is usually a family caucus where the family of the offender meets separately to work out a proposal for accountability to be brought back to the victim and the rest of the conference. The final plan must be a realistic plan of accountability that is accepted by all the participants. A modified version of this was developed by police in Australia and later in Great Britain.

What follows is an example of the dynamics of such a conference. In New Zealand, a conference was called about a young man who broke into a car, vandalized it, and took some items that were important to the owners. The victims talked about how they had been harmed. The young offender, surrounded by his family, listened. His grandfather then stood up and told the young man how he had shamed the family and the community and that he needed to make restitution to the victims, with Uncle Joe giving him a job so he could earn the money. He also needed to make things right with his family and the community. After he finished, he told his grandson that he still loved him, embraced him, and told him that he would work with him to make things right. The Maori priest also talked about how the offender was going to work in the temple. The victims were vindicated and received restitution. In fact, they came away forgiving the young man who apologized in his own way, but made it real by agreeing to do restitution. The offender accepted his accountability. There was a sense of healing as everyone left the room.

Circles

Circles as used in courts emerged from First Nation communities in Canada. Judge Barry Stuart conducted the first peacemaking circle that was acknowledged in a legal ruling. These circles were part of what inspired me to use circles in the work I do, including grievance procedures involving ministerial wrongdoing. The United Methodist Church has affirmed restorative justice principles and practices in its Social Principles. In 2004, the church affirmed such principles and practices in its complaint process involving ministers. Responding to such complaints in a restorative way using a circle process has been the primary source of my experience with restorative justice in the church. I have facilitated circles of healing and accountability involving ministers who, for example, have stolen money or have been involved in inappropriate or abusive sexual behavior. In a facilitation of a complaint against a pastor for stealing money, the circle might include members of the church that has been harmed, the district superintendent and a member of the board of ordained ministry who represent the covenant of ministry that has been breached, the minister, and the spouse of the minister, their best friends, and an ex-offender. The circle can include a much larger group of people than a victim offender conference.

Stephanie Hixon and I decided early on in our work that a victim offender conference was inappropriate in a sexual harassment or sexual abuse case. Just having the victim and the offender present with no other support does not have the necessary protections against the power imbalance and the possibility of ongoing harm. We decided the larger circle process was appropriate with the inclusion of the support people the victim selected, with key leaders to bring wisdom to the group and deal with the breach of the covenant of ministry, and with support people for the offender. We have conducted a significant number of such circles of healing and accountability. With much preparation and consent of all the parties, remarkable work has been done in these circles.

I would add that in circles dealing with deep conflicts in a church, I have often found under the presenting issues secrets about sexual abuse or other abuse in the congregation that was never dealt with satisfactorily. Such secrets create harm and dis-ease in the community until they are surfaced and dealt with in a restorative way.

Conclusion

In Matthew 18 Jesus described the journey for those who are harmed and those who harm. Jesus gives priority to the victim as the person with the moral authority to confront, to seek accountability and healing. "If another member of the church sins against you, go and point out the fault when the two of you are alone. If the member listens to you, you have regained that one" (Matt. 18:15). If the person who did the harm listened, he was restored to community. Listening in the Bible includes understanding, confessing, and repenting—making things right. The journey of the person who did the harm is a journey of moral responsibility—a path of conversion, accountability, and healing.

Jesus was steeped in biblical justice—an understanding of the relational nature of justice, an understanding that justice involves the fulfillment of the demands or obligations of a relationship. Jesus taught us that the journey of reconciliation is a journey of restorative justice.

Recently *The Christian Century* summarized an article from *Religion & Theology* (vol. 15), which tells a story of restorative justice in contemporary South Africa:

> Mapule Ramashala, a black South African, was verbally harassed when she moved into a white suburb. Some youths tried to burn down her house. But after police arrested 12 youths for the crime Ramashala refused to press charges. Instead, she met with the parents of the youths, telling them that she assumed they would organize the community to help her rebuild her house. She arranged for the youths who were charged with arson to perform community service. And she met with them periodically to see what was happening in their lives and to check on their progress in school. The community rallied around the task of restoring Ramashala's house and came to accept her into the community.[8]

TEN

Healing the Community and Creating a Culture of JustPeace

Be well together.

෨ஒ෴

Celebrate each step toward communal healing.
Be prayerful, persistent, and patient.

The ultimate goal of all our preparation and engagement for conflict transformation and peacebuilding is to find healing in our relationships, to flourish in community, to *be well together*. It involves more than just addressing a single conflict. It is about creating a different way of living together, a culture of *justpeace*. In this final chapter, I share where my own search for a better way of dealing with conflict came to rest—where I found *healing power* and a *place, a time, a ritual*, where we can be well together. I have talked about the importance of getting people to a table where they can engage one another and work together to address the issues, the harm, and the problems that divide them. For me, that table is the Table of Holy Communion.[1]

Much of what we have learned about conflict transformation and peacebuilding is summed up in this central ritual of the Christian faith. This ritual can create and inform a powerful space for a circle to do its work. At the end of a circle process, Holy Communion can be, for Christians, a closing ritual affirming relational healing that has occurred or the support we need to continue to live together in our brokenness.

As I said at the outset, my friends who are Muslims and Jews, for example, have been most inspirational to me when they speak out of their own rituals and primary language. I am going to share here with all my friends the deepest lessons of my journey in faith as a Christian, believing that this is the greatest gift I can offer, knowing that others will share with me the rituals where they find deepest meaning.

The Healing Power of the Host

The essential power of this Table is that the One who reconciles and heals is the Host of this Table. I believe that the One in whom I have experienced God incarnate is present at all tables, but here at this Table, we recognize the Host and consciously open ourselves to this One. We set the Table, we provide space for everyone at the Table, but we are not the One who has the power to heal. At this Table we celebrate the reality that we do not have to be the fixer or the healer, but we can be peacebuilders, children of God, gratefully dependent on the healing power of God, as described in chapter 4. We can and should be the conduits for the healing work of the Host. In chapter 2, we recognized that we needed to open our heart and mind to God's love, as incarnate in Jesus, reducing our anxiety and drawing us toward reconciliation and being a reconciler. This Table is the central place where we communally open ourselves to the healing, reconciling love of God as experienced in the life, death, and resurrection of Jesus whom we call the Christ. He is the one who broke down the walls of hostility (Eph. 2:14). He is the one through whom God reconciled the world to God's self, not counting our trespasses. This is a Table of relational healing, restorative justice, and reconciliation.

The Liturgy: The Spiritual Formation of Peacebuilders

Chapter 6 spoke about the power of ritual to form us. The liturgy of Holy Communion concerns the formation of peacebuilders. As we celebrate at the Table we are formed into reconcilers. Think about the power of this reality. We are not talking about a workshop for a few people in a few places. We are talking about the possibility of weekly or monthly formation in churches throughout the world! What if we understood Communion as formation for peacebuilding and allowed ourselves to be so formed? We would have a grassroots peace movement that would be global and massive. Let's look at what I mean by the content of the liturgy. I have chosen the liturgy of the United Methodist Church as an example.[2] It begins with an invitation to all who "seek to live in peace with one another." We know that the early church took seriously the admonition by Jesus:

> So when you are offering your gift at the altar, if you remember that your brother or sister has something against you, leave your gift there before the altar and go; first be reconciled to your brother or sister, and then come and offer your gift. (Matt. 5:23-24)

What if we again took this seriously as we prepared for Holy Communion and did what we could before we came to the Table to be reconciled with the brother or sister who has something against us? Such action would better prepare us for responding to the invitation. We would show by our action that we do want to live in peace with one another.

The message of Holy Communion is of God's forgiveness and steadfast love in spite of our failure to love God and neighbor. Our prayer of confession includes "we have rebelled against your love, we have not loved our neighbors. . . . Forgive us, we pray." In response to our confession, we are told we are forgiven.

At the heart of the liturgy lies the good news of God's everlasting love and forgiveness in spite of our failures. At this Table we see ourselves as a forgiven people who are called to the spiritual practice of forgiveness as described in chapter 3. In fact, we are asked to work beyond forgiveness to reconciliation, as we hear the invitation to "offer one another signs of reconciliation and love" in the section called The Peace. The instruction is: "All exchange signs and words of God's peace." This is the one time in worship we are told to get up out of our seats and reach out to others. Have you been part of a service where someone actually went beyond "good morning" to reach across the aisle to someone with whom he or she was in conflict? When I ask this question in presentations about the liturgy of Holy Communion, not many hands go up, but some do. I've heard stories of remarkable, life-changing, congregation-transforming events. When people truly do reach out to reconcile with another, it can transform not only the people involved but also the whole congregation.

Through the Great Thanksgiving we enter into God's salvation history. We will talk about the remembrance of the actions of Jesus at the Last Supper in a later section of this chapter. Appropriately, we begin with gratitude. "It is right to give our thanks and praise." A grateful spirit is at the heart of chapter 7, our study of appreciative inquiry. The key theological grounding for appreciative inquiry is found in the first act of God: "You formed us in your image and breathed into us the breath of life."

We next recognize that we need to face the fact that we have fallen short of God's plan for creation—we have turned away from God, our love has failed, and we find ourselves in captivity to our own idolatry. We hear themes similar to those in chapters 8 and 9, about facing the problems as well as the harm. We hear themes about relational covenants (chapter 6), recognizing that God is a God who has made covenant with us and calls us back to the covenant relationship through the prophets. We learn, as we discussed in chapter 1, that we do not need to fear, for God is with us and will deliver us.

Next we hear about the work of Jesus in God's salvation history. The work of Jesus is the work of liberation, healing, restorative justice, and reconciliation. The covenant is open to all. The goal of God's salvation history is summed up in these words: "By your Spirit make us one with Christ, one with each other, and one in ministry to all the world, until Christ comes in final victory and we feast at his heavenly banquet."

As observed in chapter 2, life is all about relationships—with God and neighbor. It is ultimately about being one together at a feast where we are all fed and where we all flourish.

The invitation is to those who seek to live in peace with one another. We are then sent out with the admonition to "go forth in peace." We are able to do so because of the grace, the love, and the communion that goes with us.

What if we as Christians took this liturgy seriously? What if we opened ourselves every week to be formed by it into the ministers of reconciliation, the peacebuilders, we are called to be?

Breaking the Cycles of Violence and Retribution

No one at this Table is unaware of the destructive conflicts in our world, in our communities, in the workplace, and in our homes. We bring all these conflicted worlds to the Table. The greatest issue of our day is how we are going to break out of the cycles of retribution and violence that are tearing our world and our relationships apart. At the Table of Holy Communion, each time we commune, we are reminded that the only way out of these cycles is through the path of forgiveness. At this Table we celebrate the defeat of the powers of retribution and violence through the Word of Forgiveness from the Cross and through the Resurrection. We see the heart and soul of our theology as developed in chapters 2 and 3. We finally are freed to give up the idolatry that violence is redemptive, that it will save us. What better place to bring our conflicts? What transformation might we offer the world if at the Table and from the Table we showed the world the path of forgiveness?

A Place of Higher Ground

Most of us at the Table are not oblivious to the deep conflicts in our churches; some may center on the meaning of Holy Communion itself. Walter Brueggemann says, "It is around that table that we have had our greatest conflicts because we know intuitively that in eating and drinking we are choosing our brand of shalom and legitimating an ordering of our world."[3] Divisions on a variety of issues can reach the point where some even talk of schism. One of the toughest problems in the work of conflict transformation is how to get people who disagree to the table. At the Table of Holy Communion, we find ourselves all standing together, regardless of our differences. I have a growing conviction that on some issues we are not, at least in the near term, going to find common ground, but we can find at the Table higher ground, transcendent ground to which we are invited and where we can stand together. What better place to bring our conflicts, especially those that seem intractable? What would the body of Christ look like for the world if we began to celebrate this gift and this reality of higher ground, instead of being focused on our differences?

The Table of Good News

The Table is the table of the good news that we are reconciled with God and that we can be reconcilers. In United Methodism, we, with John Wesley, believe that Holy Communion is a converting ordinance, not merely a confirming ordinance.[4] We do not share in Holy Communion because of our worthiness. We come out of our hunger to receive God's gracious love, to receive forgiveness and healing. It is not a reward for penance and merit but a means by which God transforms us more fully into God's image. It is a means of grace. The Table is the table of vulnerability where I can come "just as I am." The Table is a place where we can be authentic and truthful, where God knows us and "no secrets are hidden." This is a Table where our needs, as described in chapter 8, are fully known. What better place to bring our conflicts? This sacred space becomes a safe space for engaging our conflicts well.

A Table of Interconnection and Interdependence

At this table, in the words of Walter Brueggemann, holiness is seen as "relational engagement," not separation.[5] As John Wesley said, "The Gospel of Christ knows no religion but social, no holiness, but social holiness."[6] Here we understand our interconnection and interdependence. We need each other. The Table is a place of accountability to God, to each other, to the cosmos. It is a Table of restorative justice, of healing. What better place to bring our conflicts? The Table is a banquet table placed in the presence of our enemies. This is a Table of abundance, not scarcity, for the whole of the cosmos.

Is this the way, however, that we actually experience communion? Are we among those who try to avoid Holy Communion Sunday because we do not see its meaning or because it causes the service to go too long, interfering with our luncheon plans? Do we see the ritual as primarily food for me and not food for the community and the world? Do we experience it only as individualistic and self-serving, or truly as relational and communal?

The first-person pronouns throughout the liturgy are consistently plural—"we," "us," "our." Part of Paul's condemnation of the eucharistic practices of the Corinthian church is that they do not wait for the rest of the community to gather, and they do not share their food (see 1 Cor. 11:21, 33). Is our Table one of the most segregated and exclusive tables we experience in our lives? We say in the United Methodist Church that the Table is an open table, open to all. How do we make this a reality?

The Lessons of the Last Supper

The most important lesson for me about the Table has come through studying what Jesus did at the Last Supper, the meal we are called to remember. This lesson has led to the conviction that the Table might become transforming and formative for us and for the world when we begin to recognize, with Jesus, that the Table is a place to name and engage our conflicts and practice reconciliation.

The Context: Conflict

To set the stage, we know that this meal we call the Last Supper is related in some way to Passover and the remembrance of slavery and exodus from Egypt. "Passover" relates to the action of God in passing over and smiting the firstborn in Egypt (Exod. 12:12) or passing over and sparing the "houses of the Israelites in Egypt" (Exod. 12:27). The context was the enslavement of the people of Israel and their ultimate liberation or exodus. Significant conflict!

We also know that this supper takes place in Jerusalem. Jesus is aware that certain religious and political forces in Jerusalem want to kill him. He does not head for the hills, nor does he join the zealots to fight. In fact, he courageously enters the eye of the storm on a donkey. As we noted in chapter 1, the primary way of dealing with conflict in our churches is avoidance, "heading for the hills." In our world, we know that ultimately we take up the sword, believing violence will save us, that violence can be redemptive. Jesus rejects both flight and fight. He chooses a third way.

So, the context of the Last Supper is conflict, recognized historically through the celebration of Passover and through the present reality for Jesus and his disciples in Jerusalem.

A Meal

Meals, times of nourishment, relationship, and communion, are key events in the life of Jesus. In many ways, Jesus defines his ministry around meals and the people with whom he shares them. He eats with sinners, with Gentiles, and with tax collectors. His enemies noticed this practice, which was part of their complaint against him. Jesus created conflict by his eating habits. His table fellowship was a living parable of forgiveness. His meals were banquets, recognition of the abundance of creation and the unlimited nature of love and nurture as seen in the feeding of the five thousand. This table of abundance is set in the presence of his enemies. This meal is at the end of a long journey for Jesus, similar to the journey in the Twenty-third Psalm. Through the "darkest valley" he comes to the table in the midst of and in the presence of his enemies. This Table is ultimately a table of restoration and reconciling encounter, and he gives a cup that overflows. In the midst of the life and death conflict in which

Jesus finds himself, Jesus moves to bring his disciples, including Judas, around him for one last supper. This Table is a table for a meal, not an altar.

Naming the Conflicts at the Table

After the disciples have taken their places and are eating, what are the first words Jesus said? According to the Gospel of Mark, he said, "Truly I tell you, one of you will betray me, one who is eating with me." He added, "It is one of the twelve, one who is dipping bread into the bowl with me" (Mark 14:17-20). Isn't this startling? What a way to start a dinner party! At his final dinner with his disciples, the first words of Jesus name the conflict that is the elephant in the room. Judas is going to betray Jesus. We see in John's Gospel the other way that Jesus names the conflict in which he found himself, the conflict written deep into the whole social fabric of his day. He moves from the head of the table to the foot of the table, takes the place of the least and washes the feet of all the disciples (John 13:3-17). In doing so, he names the structural and systemic problem of his society. He turns the society upside down.

In John's Gospel, Jesus also names the denial and abandonment he will experience. Peter, the one on whom the future church would be founded, asked, "Lord, why can I not follow you now? I will lay down my life for you." Jesus answered, "Will you lay down your life for me? Very truly, I tell you, before the cock crows, you will have denied me three times" (John 13:37-38). Jesus says in Mark, "You will all become deserters" (Mark 14:27). Abandonment, more than betrayal, is what most of us do. We do not feel we need God. We do not have the courage to follow God's way.

There is nothing sentimental or individualistic or pietistic about this meal. The meal is not privatized or spiritualized. There is nothing here that is romantic or escapist. At this Table we experience the real world, with real and deep conflict. Jesus sits at his last supper, under the shadow of the cross with the man who would betray him and eleven others who will desert him. Does that experience sound conflicted to you? And Jesus named it. Justice requires the naming. Truth requires the naming. Transformation requires the naming. What is unnamed lies just beneath the surface. It often develops dis-ease. It gets worse until it explodes in very destructive ways. You must name it to heal it. Diagnosis is necessary for treatment. The naming, for Jesus, was the only way to begin the process of transforming this conflict into something constructive, into a new covenant, into a new revelation. The naming also helps us to understand the significance of the bread and wine. In the naming, we begin to see our need. We experience our hunger. We feel our thirst. We know we need God and each other. We need to be reconciled and to be a reconciler.

Giving Bread and Wine

What Jesus does next is remarkable, radical, and transforming in the context of his day and ours. After naming the conflict, he turns and offers everyone—Judas, Peter, everyone—bread and wine. Think about this gesture. He reaches over to Judas and gives him a portion of a loaf he has blessed, not cursed, and says to Judas, "Take; this is my body." He also gives this bread to Peter and all the others who would deny him. Then he takes a cup, and after giving thanks, he gives it to them, and all of them drink from it—*all* means Judas as well as Peter. He says, "This is my blood of the covenant, which is poured out for many" (Mark 14:22-24). The bread is the symbol of God's sustaining God's creation, best symbolized by the manna in the wilderness. The wine is a sign of the heavenly banquet (see 1 Cor. 11:23-26; Matt. 26:26-29). It is a sign of the new covenant between God and God's people—a covenant of forgiveness and reconciliation. The one cup symbolizes the unity of the body in Christ gathered at the table. Jesus names the conflict, but not in order to give a stone or to set the stage for retribution and punishment. He names it and then gives bread and wine. Indeed, he gives his life. Here Jesus reframes our whole reality and the way we are to respond to conflict, differences, and harm. This is a different reality than the temptation in the wilderness where "the tempter came and said to him, 'If you are the Son of God, command these stones to become loaves of bread'" (Matt. 4:3). This reframing is a different reality from the world of Judas and the reality of our world, a different way to deal with betrayal and harm. This reframing is a different way of dealing with violence, where you name the harm and give bread to your enemy. You name the conflict and respond with the gift of forgiveness. Think of what he has done with bread and wine, whose ingredients have gone through a process of being beaten, ground, and trodden underfoot. This act of giving bread and wine is the symbolic act of forgiveness written deep in the Last Supper.

The frame within which Jesus calls us to live out our lives is not the frame of naming to punish, but the frame of naming to give bread. At this Table I began to find the fullest response to my search for a better way than the adversarial retributive model. Here we move from blaming to naming, from punishment to accountability, from retribution to forgiveness. The naming becomes a different reality in the context of the gift of bread and forgiveness. When the second step in the process after naming is giving bread, the tone of the naming is changed. It does not have the tone of blaming or humiliation. It does not have the "feel" of a statement to punish or wound or humiliate or dismiss. It creates a difference in the speaker and in the hearer. It opens up a different spirit in the speaker. It opens up in the hearer, in large part because of this different spirit, the possibility of openness to real accountability as opposed to a purely defensive response. There is a judgment here, but it is the judgment of love.

At this Table Jesus models speaking the truth in love and using our imaginations (see chapter 3). At this Table Jesus expands our understanding of restorative justice (see chapter 9). The giving of bread does not negate the reality that our deeds have consequences, that accountability is important. Jesus says at the Last Supper, "The Son of Man goes as it is written of him, but woe to that one by whom the Son of Man is betrayed! It would have been better for that one not to have been born" (Mark 14:21). We read in Matthew that Judas recognized his sin, threw down the pieces of silver in the Temple, and hanged himself (Matt 27:3-5). There are consequences for our actions. Some actions are so contrary to God's plan for life that it would have been better for the actor not to have been born. However, none of this is seen here as God's or Jesus' retribution against Judas. The hanging is self-imposed. The naming and the giving of bread have the potential of making all things new. Was Jesus reaching out to Judas and giving him the opportunity to reconsider his plan? In the garden of Gethsemane, according to one translation, he said to Judas, "Why are you here?" (Matt 26:50, CEV). There is in this statement a sense that Judas, after the supper, might not have betrayed Jesus. Judas was given the opportunity of a new life. Jesus has transformed both the way we deal with conflict, differences, and harm as well as the way we experience Holy Communion.

Remembering Jesus' Last Supper as we participate in the ritual of Holy Communion, we see the Table as a place where we receive the gift of communal as well as personal forgiveness. We are also called to forgive. We see the Table as the place where we receive the word of reconciliation but also where we are spiritually formed into reconcilers, empowered to name and give bread, empowered to practice reconciliation. As Paul says, "Everything has become new! All this is from God, who reconciled us to himself through Christ, and has given us the ministry of reconciliation; that is, in Christ God was reconciling the world to himself, not counting their trespasses against them, and entrusting the message of reconciliation to us" (2 Cor. 5:17-19). What might it look like if we truly remembered and deeply internalized the lessons of the Last Supper? What might this mean for our practice of Holy Communion? What might this mean for the way we live our lives together? In addition to affecting our life away from the Table, what if we could somehow find times to name our conflicts at the Table, practice the ministry of reconciliation at the Table, and give bread to each other? More important, what might this mean for our world if this Table truly becomes a place of healing and reconciliation?

I am reminded of a story from the South African Truth and Reconciliation Commission. In the days of apartheid, seven youth were killed by the South African military in an ambush. One of the men who participated in executing the youth testified before the Commission. In the room were the mothers of these young men. After he finished testifying, the mothers were asked if they wanted to say anything. The spokeswoman for the group of mothers said that they did want to speak. She turned to the young man and said, "You are going to listen to our anger. Sit there and listen." One after another, these mothers spoke of the pain they had suffered. Then, after all had finished talking, one of the mothers turned to the man, who was totally crushed, and said, "Come here. Come here; let me hold you. Let me forgive you. I have no son, now. But I want you to be my son, so that you will never do these things again." She named the conflict. She then offered bread—indeed, her life.

Practice at the Table

In those circumstances where we fail to reconcile after leaving our gifts at the altar (Matt. 5:23-24), what if we brought the person we should seek out and be reconciled with to the Table, where we could, in the presence and with the assistance of others in the community, listen to each other's stories, experience each others joys and sorrows, and pursue the journey of reconciliation together in community?

An Episcopal priest, who is a faculty colleague, noted recently that Episcopalians have always celebrated Communion weekly, and he has not seen it make an appreciable difference in the spiritual formation and practice of his parishioners. He liked the idea of engaging our conflicts at the Table as a way of opening up the meaning and the formative power of the Table. I have come to believe that, if we can engage our conflicts at the Table in the context of Holy Communion, this meal can become the most powerful, healing ritual known to humankind, especially when we bring to the Table the lessons we have learned from the field of conflict transformation. This perspective on Holy Communion might be new to you, but it is grounded in Jesus' actions and teaching at the Last Supper.

What might it mean for us to name our conflicts at the Table, work through the conflicts to a good place, and do so with the understanding that we would then receive and share bread and wine? I am not describing a process that would take place on Sunday morning in the context of an hour-long worship service of Holy Communion. The circle of Holy Communion might take place on a Wednesday night, when we have the time to work through our problems and our harm. My hope is that these experiences, however, will begin to inform the Table on Sunday morning, when the people remember the times when the Table was the context for relational healing. My hope is that these experiences begin to inform all the tables in our lives. I am describing a process within the community of Christians. I hope this process might inform other tables where we come together to seek a good place with our neighbors regardless of their religious affiliation. Finally, I should point out two primary challenges to what I am suggesting about practice at the Table. The first challenge is not to make this holy mystery, which is a work of salvation, simply a tool or a formulaic means to an end. We need to recognize that this is God's Table of Reconciliation, while recognizing that God has prepared it for us and God calls us at this Table to be reconcilers. The second challenge is to do no harm to victims and offenders at the Table by using the ritual to be manipulative or coercive, to force them to forgive or to reconcile when they are not ready. We need to keep both of these challenges in mind as we try to practice reconciliation at the Table.

What does the practice look like? After a greeting that recognizes each person and the courage and hope that brought them to the Table and after naming what the focus of our conversation will be, we recognize that we are at the Table of Holy Communion. The Table is set with the cup and the bread. We recognize we are in the presence of the One who loves each one of us, who forgives, who reconciles and who can guide us in the challenging journey of dealing with our own conflicts and experiences of harm. We talk about the *Invitation,* about how we are at the Table because we would like to live in peace with each other, recognizing how hard this can be and that this peace must be a just peace. We recognize that we are going to confess the way we are by sharing our stories with each other before God. We agree together that, regardless of the outcome, at the end of our time together we will receive the gift of the bread and wine, needing it as much if we fail as we do if we succeed. We pray for guidance. Being in this sacred space, in most situations, immediately creates a different and more constructive dynamic in the circle.

We then close our circle with Holy Communion, even if we were not able truly to offer each other signs of reconciliation and love. This ritual must be done in a way that is not manipulative and does not trivialize either people's harm or the sacrament of Holy Communion. All ritual is highly contextual, depending on the focus for the circle at the Table.

This book is filled with different examples of conflicted situations that might be brought to the Circle of Holy Communion. Our church had such a circle. A family was having problems dealing with the drug addiction of their son. They expressed the need for help. Members of the community came together around the Table. Everything was named. Everything was discussed. Members of the church became part of this family's healing journey, agreeing in different ways to help. Everyone found their lives and issues were being touched in healing ways as well. The nonparty participants talked about how they were helped by the process, how they were moved to deeper levels within themselves as they considered their own woundedness and as they walked with those who asked for healing at the Table.

I have participated in difficult conversations around the Table—on issues that have created deep wounds. I have participated in circles of healing and accountability around the Table where ministers have stolen money or where sexual abuse has taken place. I have found that the higher ground of the Table provides a different tone and openness on the part of all the participants. The Table has been a source of healing for the participants.

Breaking Down the Walls and Coming to the Table

On Worldwide Communion Sunday at Salem United Methodist Church in Harlem, where I served as an intern, I witnessed the matriarch of the congregation pounding on each wall of the church saying, "We need to break down the walls of this church so that everyone can come to the Table of our Lord." This Table is not only for our church, but it is also for the communities and the world in which we live.

I have a dream, a dream for your church. When people walk by your church, you will hear them say: "Inside this church is a healing, restoring table. At this table, you truly hear and experience the good news of God's love and forgiveness. You find people living out the call to a ministry of reconciliation. At this table, you can be authentic, including dealing with your hurt and your conflicts. Conflicts are named, not in the spirit of punishment but in the spirit of getting to a good place together. My friend came to a good place with his family at this table. Another friend came to a good place with his neighbor with whom he had been feuding. Folks gather around this table to discuss the major issues of the day and to discern what God's love is calling us to do. This table has become the center every Sunday of weekly celebrations of restoration, healing, and reconciliation. Everything becomes new at this table. I want to be a part of this place with this table. At this table we can be well together." In my dream, your church has created, around this table, a culture of *justpeace*.

Concluding Principles

Be prayerful. We need help! We need to keep ourselves open to the guidance of the One who reconciles, heals, and restores. We need to pray for each person in a conflict and for ourselves as well. Such prayer opens our imagination and creativity. Such prayer can help us be a conduit for the healing work of God.

Be persistent. Miracles happen. Nothing in all creation can separate us from the love of God. The last word is the Resurrection, not the Crucifixion. Every step toward healing, reconciliation, and *justpeace* should be celebrated.

Be patient. In a society that encourages adversarial processes for "managing conflict," this is countercultural work. Be patient with yourself and others. Just getting people to the table is a real accomplishment. "Love does not resolve every conflict. It accepts conflict as the arena in which the work of Love is to be done."[7]

A Summary

Prepare Yourself for Conflict Transformation

Create a well, not a wall.
Create in yourself an openness to conflict as a natural and necessary
part of God's creation, an opportunity for growth and revelation.

Allow the well to fill.
Open your heart and mind to God's love, drawing you toward
reconciliation and being a reconciler.

Be well prepared.
Be prepared to listen for understanding, speak the truth in love,
use your imagination, and practice forgiveness.

Be well. Be a well.
Be a mediating presence in the midst of conflict.

Engage Others in Conflict Transformation

Create a common well together.
Design a circle process for a good conversation to get
to a better place together.

Share the well.
Together open yourselves to God through ritual and to each other
through a relational covenant.

Appreciate the life-giving waters.
Elicit stories of peak experiences, grace-filled moments, and dreams
of a preferred future.

Go beneath the surface.
Move from positions to interests and needs,
generating options to reach consensus.

Drink deeply the healing waters.
Move from retribution to restoration: healing the harm, affirming
accountability, and creating a new relationship.

Be well together.
Celebrate each step toward communal healing.
Be prayerful, persistent, and patient.

To learn more about JustPeace
Center for Mediation and Conflict, visit

http://www.justpeaceumc.org

NOTES

PROLOGUE

1. John Paul Lederach created the word *justpeace* and started a movement to have it accepted as a dictionary entry by 2050. The JustPeace Center for Mediation and Conflict Transformation of the United Methodist Church is part of this movement. See "Justpeace: The Challenge of the 21st Century" in *People Building Peace: Platform for Conflict Prevention and Transformation*. 1999. Available online at http://www.gppac.net/documents/pbp_f/part1/1_justpe.htm

2. C. Kirk Hadaway, *FACTS on Growth: A New Look at the Dynamics of Growth and Decline in American Congregations Based on the Faith Communities Today 2005 National Survey of Congregations* (Hartford, CT: Hartford Institute for Religious Research, Hartford Seminary, 2006), 16.

3. Howard Zehr, *The Little Book of Restorative Justice* (Intercourse, PA: Good Books, 2002), 37.

4. Margaret J. Wheatley, *Turning to One Another: Simple Conversations to Restore Hope to the Future* (San Francisco: Berrett-Koehler Publishers, 2002), 3.

5. Jonathan Sacks, *The Dignity of Difference: How to Avoid the Clash of Civilizations* (New York: Continuum, 2002), 2.

6. Ronald S. Kraybill with Alice Frazer Evans and Robert A. Evans, *Peace Skills: A Manual for Community Mediators* (San Francisco: Jossey-Bass, 2001), 5.

7. Daniel Day Williams, Lecture, Union Theological Seminary, New York City, 1968.

8. JustPeace Center for Mediation and Conflict Transformation. http://www.justpeaceumc.org

9. Religion and Conflict Transformation Program at Boston University School of Theology. http://www.bu.edu/rct/

CHAPTER 1 CHANGING OUR ATTITUDE TOWARD CONFLICT

1. Reinhold Niebuhr, *The Nature and Destiny of Man*, vol. 1, *Human Nature* (New York: Charles Scribner's Sons, 1941), 182.

2. Walter Wink, *The Powers That Be: Theology for a New Millennium* (New York: Doubleday, 1998), 42.

3. Robert Frost, "Mending Walls" in *The Poetry of Robert Frost: The Collected Poems, Complete and Unabridged*, ed. Edward Connery Lathem (New York: Henry Holt and Company, 1969), 33.

4. Adam Curle, *Making Peace* (London: Tavistock Publications, 1971).

5. For those who want to further explore their default position, see Speed B. Leas, *Discover Your Conflict Management Style*, rev. ed. (Bethesda, MD.: Alban Institute, 1997).

6. Parker J. Palmer, "The Broken-Open Heart: Living with Faith and Hope in the Tragic Gap," *Weavings: A Journal of the Christian Spiritual Life* 24, no. 2, (March/April 2009):7–8.

7. Wink, *The Powers That Be*, 166–67.

8. Walter Wink, *Engaging the Powers: Discernment and Resistance in a World of Domination* (Minneapolis: Fortress Press, 1992), 263.

9. Wink, *The Powers That Be*, 168–72.

10. Henry Wadsworth Longfellow, quoted in *The Chautauquan* 4 (October 1883–July 1884):211.

CHAPTER 2 DISCOVERING A THEOLOGY OF CONFLICT TRANSFORMATION

1. See Willard M. Swartley, *Covenant of Peace: The Missing Peace in New Testament Theology and Ethics* (Grand Rapids, MI: William B. Eerdmans Publishing Company, 2006).

2. See Clarence Jordan, *Sermon on the Mount* (Valley Forge, PA: Judson Press, 1952), 17–35.

3. Roberta C. Bondi's paraphrase of *Dorotheos of Gaza: Discourses and Sayings*, trans. Eric P. Wheeler (Kalamazoo, MI: Cistercian Publications, 1977), 138–39, in *Memories of God: Theological Reflections on a Life* (Nashville: Abingdon Press, 1995), 201.

4. Ibid.

5. John Paul Lederach, *The Moral Imagination: The Art and Soul of Building Peace* (New York: Oxford University Press, 2005), 34.

6. Lynn Margulis and Dorion Sagan, *Microcosmos: Four Billion Years of Evolution from Our Microbial Ancestors* (New York: Summit Books/Simon and Schuster, 1986), 14–15.

7. Margaret J. Wheatley, *Leadership and the New Science: Discovering Order in a Chaotic World*, 2nd ed. (San Francisco: Berrett-Koehler Publishers, 1999), 11.

8. See Beverly Harrison, *Justice in the Making: Feminist Social Ethics* (Louisville, KY: Westminster John Knox Press, 2004), in which she continues to develop her relational theology.

9. Carter Heyward, *Saving Jesus from Those Who Are Right: Rethinking What It Means to Be Christian* (Minneapolis: Fortress Press, 1999), 62.

10. Martin Buber, *I and Thou,* trans. Walter Kaufmann (New York: Charles Scribner's Sons, 1970), 59, 62.

11. Ibid., 123.

12. Desmond Mpilo Tutu, *No Future Without Forgiveness* (New York: Image/ Doubleday, 1999), 31.

13. Buber, *I and Thou,* 69.

14. Ibid., 112–13.

15. Sacks, *The Dignity of Difference,* 50–51, 53.

16. Ibid., 20–21.

17. Ibid., 23.

18. Chiara Lubich, *Jesus: The Heart of His Message, Unity and Jesus Forsaken* (Hyde Park, NY: New City Press, 1985), 23–24.

19. Walter Brueggemann, "Vision for a New Church and a New Century: Part II, Holiness Become Generosity," *Union Seminary Quarterly Review,* 54, nos. 1–2 (2000):57.

20. Ibid., 59.

CHAPTER 3 LEARNING RELATIONAL SKILLS

1. Dietrich Bonhoeffer, *Life Together,* trans. John W. Doberstein (New York: Harper & Row, Publishers, 1954), 97–98.

2. Elise Boulding, *One Small Plot of Heaven: Reflections on Family Life by a Quaker Sociologist* (Wallingford, PA: Pendle Hill Publications, 1989), 172.

3. Carl R. Rogers, *A Way of Being* (New York: Houghton Mifflin Company, 1980), quoted in John Stewart, *Bridges Not Walls: A Book about Interpersonal Communication,* 8th ed. (Boston: McGraw Hill, 2002), 643.

4. John Paul Lederach, *The Journey Toward Reconciliation* (Scottdale, PA: Herald Press, 1999), 156.

5. Sacks, *The Dignity of Difference,* 19.

6. Ibid., 23.

7. Walter Brueggemann, *The Prophetic Imagination,* 2nd ed. (Minneapolis: Fortress Press, 2001), 40

8. Lederach, *The Moral Imagination,* 62.

9. Oliver Wendell Holmes Jr., quoted in Stephen G. Haines, *The Complete Guide to Systems Thinking and Learning* (Amherst, MA: HRD Press, 2000), xii.

10. Lederach, *The Moral Imagination,* 37, 62.

11. Ignatius's "Presupposition" of his *Spiritual Exercises,* quoted in Raymond G. Helmick, "Seeing the Image of God in Others: Key to the Transformation of Conflicts," a lecture at St. Paul's Church, Cambridge, MA, April 21, 2007, 9.

12. Ibid.

13. Lederach, *Moral Imagination,* 5, 36.

14. Michael Lapsley, as quoted in Carolyn Yoder, *The Little Book of Trauma Healing* (Intercourse, PA: Good Books, 2005), 45.

15. Chart by Olga Botcharova from Raymond G. Helmick, SJ, and Rodney L. Petersen, eds. *Forgiveness and Reconciliation: Religion, Public Policy, and Conflict Transformation* (Philadelphia: Templeton Foundation Press, 2001), 298.

16. Viktor Frankl, *Man's Search for Meaning*, rev. ed. (New York: Simon and Schuster, 1984).

17. Beverly Wildung Harrison, *Making the Connections: Essays in Feminist Social Ethics*, ed. Carol S. Robb (Boston: Beacon Press, 1985).

18. Yoder, *Little Book of Trauma Healing*, 55.

19. L. Gregory Jones, *Embodying Forgiveness: A Theological Analysis* (Grand Rapids, MI: William B. Eerdmans Publishing Co., 1995), xii.

CHAPTER 4 BECOMING PEACEBUILDERS

1. See also Mark 9:36-37; 10:15, 43-44; Luke 9:46-48, 18:17; John 3:3-5.

2. Walter Wink, *The Powers That Be*, 39.

3. Ron Kraybill, *Restoring Those Who Heal Others: Spirituality and Self-Care for Those in Danger of Burnout* (Intercourse, PA: Good Books, forthcoming), 53.

4. Albert Schweitzer quoted in Norman Cousins, *Anatomy of an Illness as Perceived by the Patient: Reflections on Healing and Regeneration* (New York: Bantam Books, 1981), 69.

5. Heyward, 62.

6. Kraybill, *Peace Skills*, 20.

7. Ibid.

8. Parker J. Palmer, *Let Your Life Speak: Listening for the Voice of Vocation* (San Francisco: Jossey-Bass, 2000), 64.

9. Jim Stutzman and Carolyn Schrock-Shenk, eds., *Mediation and Facilitation Training Manual: Foundations and Skills for Constructive Conflict Transformation*, 3rd ed. (Akron, PA: Mennonite Conciliation Service, 1995), 24.

10. Carl R. Rogers quoted in Harold S. Kushner, *How Good Do We Have to Be? A New Understanding of Guilt and Forgiveness* (Boston: Little, Brown and Company, 1996), 7.

11. Robert J. Miller, ed. *The Complete Gospels: Annotated Scholars Version*, rev. ed. (San Francisco: Polebridge Press/HarperSanFrancisco, 1994), 67.

12. Stutzman and Schrock-Shenk, eds., *Mediation and Facilitation*, 24.

13. Kraybill, *Restoring Those Who Heal Others*, 70–71.

CHAPTER 5 DESIGNING GOOD PROCESS: THE CIRCLE PROCESS

1. Wheatley, *Turning to One Another*, 3, back flyleaf.

2. Ibid.

3. A Native American insight quoted in Carolyn Boyes-Watson, "Healing the Wounds of Street Violence: Peacemaking Circles and Community Youth Development," *Community Youth Development Journal* 2, No. 4 (Fall 2001):18.

4. Robert A. Baruch Bush and Joseph P. Folger, *The Promise of Mediation: Responding to Conflict Through Empowerment and Recognition* (San Francisco: Jossey-Bass Publishers, 1994), 2.

5. Kay Pranis, Barry Stuart, and Mark Wedge, *Peacemaking Circles: From Crime to Community* (St. Paul, MN: Living Justice Press, 2003) and Kay Pranis, *The Little Book of Circle Processes* (Intercourse, PA: Good Books, 2005).

6. Pranis, *The Little Book of Circle Processes*, 3.

7. Web site description, www.rocainc.org/about_history.php

8. Carolyn Boyes-Watson, *Holding the Space: The Journey of Circles at Roca, Report on the Period July 2001–June 30, 2001* (Boston: Center for Restorative Justice, Suffolk University, 2002), 21.

CHAPTER 6 CREATING RITUAL AND COVENANTS

1. Tom F. Driver, *The Magic of Ritual: Our Need for Liberating Rites that Transform Our Lives and Our Communities* (San Francisco: HarperSanFrancisco, 1991), 131.

2. Marcia McFee, "Ritual Formation: Liturgical Practices and the Practice of Peacebuilding," in *Conflict and Communion: Reconciliation and Restorative Justice at Christ's Table*, ed. Thomas W. Porter (Nashville, TN: Discipleship Resources, 2006), 68.

3. Boyes-Watson, *Holding the Space*, 28.

4. Eric H. F. Law, *The Wolf Shall Dwell with the Lamb: A Spirituality for Leadership in a Multicultural Community* (St. Louis, MO: Chalice Press, 1993), 113–14.

5. Sacks, *Dignity of Difference*, 202.

CHAPTER 7 FINDING THE POSITIVE CORE: APPRECIATIVE INQUIRY

1. Diana Whitney, Claudia Liebler, and David Cooperrider, "Appreciative Inquiry in Organizations and International Development: An Invitation to Share and Learn Across Fields" in *Positive Approaches to Peacebuiding: A Resource for Innovators*, ed. Cynthia Sampson and others (Washington, D.C.: Pact Publications, 2003), 27.

2. Ibid., 27, 49.

3. T. S. Eliot, "Choruses from The Rock," 1934.

4. Peter Storey, in personal e-mail, 2009.

5. Rainer Maria Rilke, *Letters to a Young Poet*, trans. Joan M. Burnham (New York: MFJ Books, 2000), 35.

6. Elie Wiesel, *Night*, trans. Stella Rodway (New York: Bantam Books, 1960), 2–3.

7. Parker J. Palmer, *Let Your Life Speak*, 44–46.

CHAPTER 8 MEETING NEEDS: INTEREST-BASED MEDIATION

1. Roger Fisher and William Ury, *Getting to Yes: Negotiating Agreement Without Giving In*, ed. Bruce Patton, 2nd ed. (New York: Penguin Books, 1991), 4.

CHAPTER 9 ADDRESSING HARM: RESTORATIVE JUSTICE

1. Abraham J. Heschel, *The Prophets* (New York: Harper and Row, 1962), 198.

2. John W. De Gruchy, *Reconciliation: Restoring Justice* (Minneapolis, MN: Fortress Press, 2002), 40.

3. Christopher D. Marshall, *Beyond Retribution: A New Testament Vision for Justice, Crime and Punishment* (Grand Rapids, MI: William B. Eerdmans, 2001), 277.

4. James Gilligan, *Violence: Reflections on a National Epidemic* (New York: Vintage Books/Random House, 1997), 110.

5. Zehr, *Little Book of Restorative Justice*, 32–33.

6. Ibid., 35–36.

7. Allan MacRae and Howard Zehr, *The Little Book of Family Group Conferences: New Zealand Style* (Intercourse, PA: Good Books, 2004).

8. "Restorative Justice," *The Christian Century* 125, no. 24 (December 2, 2008):8.

CHAPTER 10 HEALING THE COMMUNITY AND CREATING A CULTURE OF JUSTPEACE

1. See Thomas W. Porter Jr., ed., *Conflict and Communion: Reconciliation and Restorative Justice at Christ's Table* (Nashville, TN: Discipleship Resources, 2006).

2. From "A Service of Word and Table I," *The United Methodist Hymnal* (Nashville, TN: The United Methodist Publishing House, 1989), 6.

3. Walter Brueggemann, *Peace* (St. Louis, MO: Chalice Press, 2001), 78.

4. John Wesley, Journal from November 1, 1739 to September 3, 1741: Friday, June 27, 1740.

5. Brueggemann, "Vision for a New Church and a New Century," 55.

6. John Wesley, Preface to *Hymns and Sacred Poems*, 1739.

7. Daniel Day Williams, in a lecture at Union Theological Seminary, 1968.

CPSIA information can be obtained
at www.ICGtesting.com
Printed in the USA
BVHW040554300320
576141BV00005B/2